THRONED IN HIGHEST BLISS

THRONED
IN
HIGHEST BLISS

ALAN CAIRNS

Ambassador

Contents

THRONED IN HIGHEST BLISS

Copyright © Alan Cairns 1990

First Published 1990

ISBN 0 907927 61 0

AMBASSADOR PRODUCTIONS LTD
Providence House,
16 Hillview Avenue,
Belfast, BT5 6JR, U.K.

11 Sandringham Road,
Taylors, S.C. 29687, USA

CHAPTER ONE

True Happiness

Matthew 5:1-12

T here is something unspeakably solemn about this portion of Scripture. For one thing, the speaker is none other than God Himself, the second person of the eternal Trinity, manifested in human flesh. For another, this is the longest discourse of the Lord Jesus Christ recorded in the New Testament. And then there is the content of the passage. Someone has rightly drawn attention to the fact that this Sermon on the Mount devotes much time to presenting a proper interpretation of the law of God, its spirituality and its functions. In the Old Testament God gave the law from a mountain, and here on another mount He gives His own authoritative interpretation and application of that law. Were this a topical study of mountains, it would be fitting to go on to show that on yet another mount, the mount of Calvary, God in the person of His own dear Son made a perfect atonement and satisfaction for the broken law and wrought salvation for His people.

The entire discourse covers a great variety of subjects. But as the Lord Jesus starts out He does something which every preacher should seek to emulate: He commences in a most striking manner. I know an eminent teacher of homiletics who drives home the importance of this to his students by assuring them that the only time in a sermon they can hope to have the undivided attention of all their congregation will be in the first ten seconds. They must therefore make the best possible use of it. This opinion is not very complimentary to most modern audiences, but unfortunately it is only too true in most places. So the Lord Jesus gives us a good lesson by starting out in a striking manner.

1

In Matthew 4:17 we read, "From that time Jesus began to preach, and to say, Repent: for the kingdom of heaven is at hand." Here in chapter 5 we notice that He sat down to *teach*. Joseph Parker, himself a very eminent preacher in London, said that in that city the preachers were thronged with people, but the teachers were speaking to their half-dozens. Then he said something very interesting: "I engage to take nine-tenths of any preacher's congregation away from him, or any teacher's congregation away from him, merely by telling a striking anecdote." If it was true in the days of Joseph Parker in the late 1800s, how much truer is it today when we have reached the stage in the church where people want to be entertained with a few tear-jerking stories. They do not appear to want to be taught the Word of God. The Lord Jesus sat down and *taught* them.

What a difference there is between the opening of this message and the opening of the previous message in chapter 4. Then He had cried out in the strongest tones, "Repent." In our passage the message has not changed, but the tone has. Now the Lord Jesus starts out with the word *blessed*— "Blessed are the poor in spirit." Eight more times in this opening section He says, "Blessed," and goes on to denote a particular characteristic of the blessed people. The word *blessed* simply means "happy" in the truest and highest sense of the word. Remember, this is the Son of God speaking about happiness. What we have in these first twelve verses is **the true view of a happy life.** That is what we must now consider.

All these blessings the Lord Jesus details for us are present blessings. Though some of them are enjoyed because of a glorious future prospect, they are present blessings. The Lord Jesus is not speaking to His people about what Marxists disdainfully call "pie in the sky." Thank God, this is better than pie in the sky. We do have heaven as our home for all eternity, but in the meantime we have the reality and the joy of a happy life in this present world. When the Lord pronounces a man happy, he is happy indeed. But woe to the man who has no place in this list of divine blessings. Woe to the man who has no happiness of soul, who lacks the necessary happiness which the Lord Jesus Christ here describes. The man who cannot be counted happy by the Son of God is evidently under the curse of the Lord. Christ's is the true view of a happy life. As we consider it we should carefully mark some very general and basic truths.

DECEPTIVE APPEARANCES

The first thing that really impresses itself upon us is that spiritual reality is very often far removed from temporal appearances. Every one of these things that Jesus associates with true happiness is totally unappealing to the carnal mind. For example, He said, "Blessed are the poor in spirit. . . . Blessed are they that mourn." He does not say, "Blessed are the go-getters; blessed is the man who can make the world open up before him and lay its treasures at his feet." He does not say, "Blessed are the barons of the stock exchange; blessed are the bulls in the stock market." No! He says, "Blessed are the meek," and so on down this list of divine blessings. Every single one of them is totally unappealing to the carnal mind, entirely the reverse of what the mind of man would conceive.

The people who are here described by the Lord Jesus Christ as blessed are objects of scorn in this world. They are objects of derision or at best of pity to men of the world. But the reality is absolutely different from the appearance. The people who appear to be most liable to ridicule or pity in the eyes of the world are, according to the Son of God, the people who are most highly blessed. Conversely, the people who are most blessed in the estimation of the world are most cursed in the estimation of the Lord of glory. The appearance and the reality are two very different things. Consider a couple of Scriptures.

In Zephaniah 3:12 we read, "I will also leave in the midst of thee an afflicted and poor people." But notice what follows: "They shall trust in the name of the LORD." There is their blessing. Psalm 125:1, 2 assures us, "They that trust in the LORD shall be as mount Zion, which cannot be removed, but abideth for ever. As the mountains are round about Jerusalem, so the LORD is round about his people from henceforth even for ever." These afflicted and poor people are blessed, trusting in the name of the Lord. In verse 14 of chapter 3 Zephaniah instructs them, "Sing, O daughter of Zion; shout, O Israel; be glad and rejoice with all the heart, O daughter of Jerusalem." Now, how can poor and afflicted people sing in the midst of their circumstances? Verse 17 gives the answer: "The LORD thy God in the midst of thee is mighty;

he will save, he will rejoice over thee with joy; he will rest in his love, he will joy over thee with singing." An afflicted people, but, bless God, a people who were truly happy.

In contrast, look at Ezekiel 27:25-27. The Lord is here speaking against the city of Tyre, one of the great commercial centres of the ancient world. Her merchant vessels were going around the then-known world, trading with great success. They made that city the capital of the entire economic world of their day. Of Tyre the Lord says, "The ships of Tarshish did sing of thee in thy market: and thou wast replenished, and made very glorious in the midst of the seas." That was the appearance; the reality was very different. "Thy rowers [God is speaking in terms of shipping and so describes the leaders of Tyre as the rowers of her great vessels] have brought thee into great waters: the east wind hath broken thee in the midst of the seas. Thy riches, and thy fairs, thy merchandise, thy mariners, and thy pilots, thy calkers, and the occupiers of thy merchandise, and all thy men of war, that are in thee, and in all thy company which is in the midst of thee, shall fall into the midst of the seas in the day of thy ruin." Can you imagine this city? Apparently it was in the most enviable of positions, lifted to the very pinnacle of prosperity. But God says, in effect, "That is only an appearance. There is no cause for joy in Tyre, for your doom is sealed." God pronounces ruin despite the appearance of rich success.

Great appearances of ease and plenty abound here in America. This is the richest country in the world. On every hand there is evidence of rich abundance, but it does not take an expert on American life to understand that despite the appearance there is little peace in this land, little satisfaction, little true happiness. How different is the reality from the appearance! Conversely, there are places where food may be scarce and where life and limb may be in constant danger, but where the presence of God in the midst of His people, showing His strong right hand to save, imparts a peace and a joy most people here seldom experience. We have heard our friends from Lebanon tell us of their peace and happiness of heart, even though evil men often use them for target practice as they travel to and from church. Appearance and reality are two very different things.

4

POSSESSIONS DO NOT BRING HAPPINESS

We should also note that in Christ's Sermon on the Mount there is no blessing pronounced on any of those things which the world pursues most avidly. Sometimes the silences of Scripture are just as expressive and meaningful as its plain statements. The Lord Jesus Christ is giving a list of blessings, but there is no reference to wealth, or to houses, or to land, or even to physical health. Nowadays, under the influence of the Charismatic delusion, even people who ought to know better are tempted to equate the blessing of God with American dollars or with the state of their physical well-being. These things are all conspicuous by their absence from Christ's list. This is not to say that there is no blessing when the Lord meets your financial or physical needs. That would be far from the truth. But the essence of the happy life does not consist in things or in the circumstances of life. The reason is very simple—would to God that saints and sinners both would learn it—and it is this: there is nothing in this world, absolutely nothing, that can ever meet the needs of the souls of men or satisfy the desires of the heart. We are so often tied in to *things*. This is true even of professing Christians. There are countless numbers of people who are trying to spend their way into happiness. If only they can have this or that trinket, they will be happy. It is a waste of money and effort. Indeed, it is counter-productive, because things never bring happiness.

When evaluating possessions, always remember the man in Luke chapter 12 whom the Lord Jesus Christ called a fool. He had barns that were filled but yet were not large enough to hold his harvest. He had an overflow of this world's goods. In modern jargon, "he had it made." He had possessions and thought that he had all that was necessary to a happy life. Blithely he sat down to plan his retirement, which he expected to spend in unalloyed pleasure and unbroken happiness. But it was a plan that never came to fruition. The Lord Jesus said of this man, "Thou fool." Think of that. The Scripture also tells us, "Riches profit not in the day of wrath" (Prov. 11:4). And the Lord Jesus asked the question, "What shall it profit a man, if he shall gain the whole world, and lose his own soul?" (Mark 8:36). Possessions do not mean happiness. Some of the most miserable specimens of humanity today are the richest people in the world.

5

Not long ago there was a news item describing one of Hollywood's brightest stars and funniest actresses. People have paid millions to see her perform, but between her glittering engagements she lives in a virtual prison, mentally deranged and totally miserable. Possessions do not spell happiness.

WORLDLY PLEASURES DO NOT BRING HAPPINESS

Nor do the promiscuous pleasures of the world bring happiness. Reading recently through the book of Proverbs, I was much impressed by the constant warnings in the opening chapters against the adulteress, the harlot, and the strange woman. In the seventh chapter, for instance, in verses 6 through 11 we read, "At the window of my house I looked through my casement, and beheld among the simple ones, I discerned among the youths, a young man void of understanding, passing through the street near her corner; and he went the way to her house, in the twilight, in the evening, in the black and dark night: and, behold, there met him a woman with the attire of an harlot, and subtil of heart. (She is loud and stubborn; her feet abide not in her house.)"

Obviously the plain reference is to immorality. However, this harlot who is loud and stubborn is also a picture of this godless world and its enticements. Friendship with the world is described in Scripture as adultery in the sight of God. This harlot, then, is a picture of a world that is decked in glittering array to entice the unwary, to make men believe that its way is the way of pleasure, of happiness, and of satisfaction. And as the harlot catches the young man and kisses him with an impudent face and says, "I have peace offerings with me" (v. 14), so the world temptingly flaunts its illicit attractions, all the while assuring its victims, "You need not feel guilty about this. You may enter into all the pleasures of the world. Don't let those Bible-thumping preachers send you on a guilt trip. This is what you need to have. What is more, I have my peace offerings. There is nothing irreligious, nothing intrinsically anti-Biblical or anti-Christian, in going the way of worldliness and the way of the pleasures of this promiscuous age."

That is the stubborn, impudent face of the world. "This day have I payed my vows. Therefore came I forth to meet thee, diligently to seek thy face, and—[oh, what a deadly sentence!]—I have found thee" (vv. 14-15). Is there some reader, some young person, who even now can hear this awful boast, "I have found you"? Can you see the picture of that evil woman with the arm of seduction about that simple one? That is the picture of the world with its tentacles about a young man or a young woman, indeed any man or woman, whom it would lead to hell. The world sounds its death knell in your ear: "I have sought you, and I have found you." Its enticement is strong and continual, but of the one who succumbs to it God says, "He goeth after her straightway, as an ox goeth to the slaughter, or as a fool to the correction of the stocks; till a dart strike through his liver; as a bird hasteth to the snare, and knoweth not that it is for his life" (vv. 22-23).

We are living to see the fulfilment of Paul's prophetic statement in II Timothy 3:4. This is a day in which men are "lovers of pleasures more than lovers of God." Ultimately, it does not matter whether your pleasure is in itself illicit, as this immorality, or in itself apparently innocent. Some years ago I heard a young man arguing when this Scripture was quoted. He contended, "You are a Christian. You read Christian books, and you find pleasure. I read other literature that I like to read, and I obtain pleasure. We both do what we do for pleasure; so how can you condemn me?" He was missing the point. Wherever you obtain your pleasure, if it takes the place of God, it is idolatry and sin. "Lovers of pleasures more than lovers of God." This idolatry has even invaded many professed churches of Jesus Christ. In many places church services have become circuses, entertainments, anything to cater to the love of pleasure. The mission of the church of Christ is to feed the sheep, not to entertain the goats!

What is the end of this addiction to pleasure? The harlot world says, "I have sought you; I have found you." Its pleasures are enticing and promising, but if you fall for its blandishments you ignore the solemn fact that it will cost you your soul. That is what is at stake in this matter. The last verse of Proverbs 7 says, "Her house is the way to hell, going down to the chambers of death."

WORLDLY POWER DOES NOT BRING HAPPINESS

So there is no happiness in possessions or in the promiscuous pleasures of this world. And there is no happiness in the power for which men so

7

often sell their souls. The psalmist said, "I have seen the wicked in great power, and spreading himself like a green bay tree" (Psa. 37:35), and he at once went on to speak of his demise and removal. The place that knew him on earth now knows him no more forever. Think of what men have done to gain positions of power. They have sold their souls, they have wrecked their homes, they have made themselves liars and thieves, and some of them have stepped over the corpses of their murdered victims to reach a position of social, economic, or political eminence. And yet where are they? The wicked come and go. They obtain power for a while, but it brings them no real happiness either in this life or in the next.

In Luke 15 we read of rejoicing in heaven. What causes it? Do the angels rejoice when someone is elected to the United States Senate? There is not a word of that. Do they rejoice when a young man makes his way up the ladder of corporate success to become president of the company? Not a word of that. Or are they singing about the millions of dollars he has made along the way? Not a word of that either. Now, God can give any of those things to particular people to use for His glory, but the only thing they are singing about in heaven is when a poor, lost, guilty, hell-deserving sinner, away out there in the darkness, within a heartbeat of eternal hell, is reached by the almighty hand of the Saviour, lifted from the jaws of destruction, made into a saint and child of God, and secured for heaven for all eternity. That is what makes the angels rejoice. Anything short of that does not have even one single ingredient of true happiness in it.

TRUE HAPPINESS: A HEART RIGHT WITH GOD

The final truth we must note on this matter is that true happiness, therefore, depends upon a right relationship with the Lord. That is very obvious in the words of the Lord Jesus Christ in this passage. This poverty of spirit, this mourning of heart, this meekness, and this hungering and thirsting, are all in relation to the Lord. That must be understood, or we will fall into the common error of making the Sermon on the Mount teach salvation by virtue of human suffering and effort. All these characteristics are descriptions of a proper spiritual standing with the Lord. When a man is in a right relationship with the Lord, Christ pronounces him happy.

8

The first Psalm starts in the same way as this great sermon: "Blessed is the man," or—and this is much more explosive than it sounds in the English translation—"Oh, the blessednesses of the man that walketh not in the counsel of the ungodly, nor standeth in the way of sinners, nor sitteth in the seat of the scornful. But his delight is in the law of the LORD; and in his law doth he meditate day and night. And he shall be like a tree planted by the rivers of water, that bringeth forth his fruit in his season; his leaf also shall not wither; and whatsoever he doeth shall prosper." There is true happiness: a man rightly related to God. You will notice that he does not have the right human connections. He does not walk in the counsel of the ungodly. His ear is not fine-tuned to the advice of the world. He is not standing in the same pathway as sinners. He does not think the way they think. But he is rightly related to God. Oh, the blessednesses of that man! Psalm 32 gives you something of an insight into them: "Blessed is he whose transgression is forgiven, whose sin is covered. Blessed is the man unto whom the LORD imputeth not iniquity." Forgiveness, atonement, and the imputation of the righteousness of Christ—three inestimable blessings! Nothing is better fitted to produce true happiness.

When you have forgiveness, you have a conscience and a heart at peace. That is worth everything in this world. Paul said, "Godliness with contentment is great gain." To know your sins forgiven, to be able to put your head on the pillow at night and know that if God calls you into eternity you will be absent from the body and present with the Lord, is real happiness. When your conscience is no longer your accuser but is at rest because it is sprinkled with the precious blood of Jesus Christ, you possess happiness indeed. To be able to look God in the face and know that He is satisfied with that precious blood, know that He has garbed you in the garments of the righteousness of Christ and that you stand before Him purer than the creation of an angel, is the very essence of true happiness.

A MATTER OF THE HEART

Oh, the blessednesses of a man rightly related to God! But we must emphasize *rightly* related, because true religion is a matter of the heart. These words of Christ really must have struck His Jewish hearers very painfully, because the Jews had externalized their religion. They had the law. The Lord was going to explain the spirituality of that law, but they had made it into a mere series of *do's* and *don't's*. They thought that as long as they *looked* right they *were* right. I am a little afraid of modern evangelical Christians on the same score. I am particularly afraid that many of our Bible-believing churches too often make this mistake of externalizing religion. Your hair is the right length. You do not listen to rock music. You do not go to the cinema. Now, it is good and proper for a Christian to live a separated life in all these areas. Such personal separation is essential to our testimony. But it is very easy to look at the external markings and mistake them for true religion. Many who never set foot inside a cinema, or inside a dance hall, or any other den of iniquity, have perished nevertheless. True religion will make a man clean in his life, but it is not just so many *do's* and *don't' s*; it is a matter of the heart. Every one of these things of which the Lord Jesus speaks is a description of a heart that is rightly related to God—a heart that is in repentance of sin, in repudiation of sin, in love with God, and resting in total reliance on the merits of the Lord Jesus Christ. True religion is a matter of the heart.

The apostle Paul said in Romans 10:9, "If thou shalt confess with thy mouth the Lord Jesus, and shalt believe in thine heart that God hath raised him from the dead, thou shalt be saved." At this point modern man would challenge the apostle: "Paul, you have it wrong. Belief is a matter of the mind. It belongs to the intellect, not to the heart." But Paul is right and the critic wrong. The revealed truth of Scripture is "believe in thine heart"—believe with the affections, believe with the will.

Do you see what this means? If you are ever going to get to heaven, you can make as many "decisions" as you like, you can go through as many professions as you like, you can join as many churches as you like, you can be baptized as often as you like, and perish at the end. Unless your heart is circumcised by the regenerating grace of God, unless you are made a new creature who in repudiation of self and sin has embraced Jesus Christ, you must perish eternally. It is with the heart man believeth. What a painful and shocking thing to think of multitudes who imagine themselves to be evangelical Christians but who have been led to embrace a Romish-style system of works: if you do this or that you will be saved even though your heart has never been taken up with Christ. One eminent preacher, a professed Fundamentalist, has said that repentance is merely a change of mind towards sin but that it does not necessarily involve a change in behaviour. He is wrong. If you have a repentance that has never engaged your heart with Jesus Christ and has never led to a real change of life, you will perish with that repentance. It is merely the sorrow of the world. It is a repentance to be repented of. To be rightly related to God is much more than mere religious performance or profession. It is a matter of the heart.

HAPPY IN CHRIST, NOW AND FOREVER

When this religion of the heart is granted a man by the grace of God, the blessings conferred on him are such that nothing in heaven, earth, or hell—and certainly no circumstance of time—can remove them from him. What a wonderful passage this opening section of Matthew 5 is. Here are people crushed in spirit, but they are blessed. Their eyes are wet with mourning, but they are blessed. They are persecuted, hated, and reviled, but they are blessed. Do you see what the Lord Jesus is saying? "When I bless you, nothing can ever happen that can reverse the blessing."

Paul's lovely words in Romans 8 are to the same effect: "Who shall separate us from the love of Christ? shall tribulation, or distress, or persecution, or famine, or nakedness, or peril, or sword? . . . Nay, in all these things we are more than conquerors through him that loved us. For I am persuaded, that neither death, nor life, nor angels, nor principalities, nor powers, nor things present, nor things to come, nor height, nor depth, nor any other creature, shall be able to separate us from the love of God, which is in Christ Jesus our Lord." When God blesses you, no circumstance of time can ever take that blessing from you.

GUARANTEE OF ETERNAL HAPPINESS

The happy life the Lord now gives guarantees our happy life with Him for all eternity. Twice the Lord Jesus here refers to "the kingdom of heaven." It is an important phrase which we cannot now consider, but one thing must be clear. He could not say, "Yours is the kingdom of heaven" unless He were assuring you that you will actually reach heaven. Heaven, the home of the redeemed! Heaven, where we go to be with Christ! Will you be there? Where are you going for eternity? Where is the life of happiness you are seeking here on earth really leading you? If yours is the

11

happiness of those dead in sin, the mere temporary pleasure of those who give themselves to the flesh, then yours will be the end of the rich man in Luke chapter 16, who in hell lifted up his eyes, "being in torments." But if yours is the blessing of sins forgiven through the merits of Christ, if yours is a happiness that comes from a right relationship with God, then, praise God, heaven will be yours for all eternity. You will be forever with the Lord in the eternal enjoyment of true happiness. That is His guarantee.

Anything that presents itself a truly happy life but is tied in to the merely temporal and has no saving relationship with Christ now and gives no Biblical hope for heaven is a dangerous delusion. It is the opposite of true happiness and leads to everlasting misery. Perhaps your view of what a happy life is needs to be radically altered. Christ's view of true happiness is the right one. Anything else is cursed, not blessed. Make sure what you count as happiness is not merely the frenetic notions and emotions of a soul on the edge of destruction. If you would be truly blessed, seek Christ as your Saviour and Lord.

CHAPTER TWO

A Blessed People

Matthew 5:3-12

H *appiness.* Now, there is a word to conjure with. There is no more sought-after and yet no more elusive commodity than happiness. Thomas Aquinas said that blessedness was "the ultimate end." The great Puritan Thomas Watson agreed, calling it "the white [or target] every man aims to hit." I think they were right. In his own way and according to his own light and standard, every man seeks for happiness. Yet, despite the universal desire, happiness is a mark which few men hit. It is a goal which few men come near to achieving. The reason is both simple and Scriptural. Generally men want happiness without reference to God or to God's Christ. Or else they want happiness on terms other than those which the Lord has set forth. There is an old maxim in theology that he who would be made happy must first be made holy. That is exactly what the Lord Jesus Christ is teaching in the fifth chapter of Matthew. Nine times He uses the word *blessed,* or "happy," to describe His people. His message is simple and striking, and I trust we shall never forget it: **blessedness belongs to the people of God and to none else.**

THE LORD JESUS PRONOUNCES HIS PEOPLE TRULY HAPPY

His people are truly blessed, truly happy. You cannot read this portion without remarking the continual emphasis upon this word. I am afraid even Christians nowadays are apt to miss the impact of Christ's repeated use of this word *happy.* The old saying is that familiarity breeds contempt.

13

We are so well used to reading the Beatitudes that they do not affect us as they ought. But can you imagine the scene as the Lord Jesus sat down on the mountainside in the midst of His disciples? A crowd gathered and in hushed silence listened to the words of Him who spake as never man spake. Try to gauge the impact of these words. When God came down upon Mount Sinai to speak to Moses, He spoke with the frightening thunders of the law and condemnation, but when in the person of His Son He came down upon this mount to speak the word of the gospel, He said, "Blessed . . . blessed . . . blessed." In a world of misery, to a people trampled underfoot by an invading army, to a nation that had lost all its national rights and privileges, whose pride was trampled in the dust, His message was one of happiness. To a people who could look back to a great past and yet were languishing in a miserable present, Jesus said, "My people are truly blessed. My people are truly happy." As we shall see, it was with good reason that the Son of God insisted that happiness belongs to the people of God.

First and foremost, *they have Christ as their Saviour.* Happy indeed is the man who has Christ as his Saviour.

> *In land or store I may be poor,*
> *My place unknown, my name obscure;*
> *Of this I have the witness sure:*
> *O bless the Lord, I've Jesus.*
>
> *What though the world its gifts deny,*
> *I've riches more than gold can buy,*
> *The key to treasures in the sky—*
> *O bless the Lord, I've Jesus!*

Think of it! If you can say, "I have Christ," God says you are blessed indeed, whatever your situation. In Christ we are endowed with all that God's grace can provide.

All our sin is forgiven if we have Christ. "In those days, and in that time, saith the LORD, the iniquity of Israel shall be sought for, and there shall be none; and the sins of Judah, and they shall not be found: for I will pardon

14

them whom I reserve [or, I will pardon them whom I save]" (Jer. 50:20). I am glad God says that. He looks down on the people whom He has saved and washed in the precious blood of the Lord Jesus Christ and He says, "Though your sins may be sought for, they will not be found. Your iniquities will be searched for, but they will never be discovered." Thank God, when sin is put under the blood it is removed forever. "Their sins and iniquities will I remember no more." (Heb. 10:17). Happy is the man who is forever separated from his sin—whose ungodliness, iniquities, and transgressions are forgiven.

Implicit in all this is the truth that all his guilt is removed. This matter of guilt is one of the most urgent and pressing problems with which men have to deal. Behind much of the mental turmoil and many of the broken hearts and homes that are such a large part of modern society there is this awful, despairing thing called guilt. What can you do about it? The answer is *nothing*. You may ignore it. You may try to quiet the awful voice of accusation within you. You may determine to do better in the future. But none of this will ever change the guilt that rises before you like a mountain, forever obscuring your view of anything bright. It is like a weight that weighs upon the heart and that destroys every ounce of blessedness within the soul. That is the problem of guilt. But, thank God, those who have Christ have a Justifier who removes all guilt so that we can say, in the words of the thirty-second Psalm, "Blessed is he whose transgression is forgiven, whose sin is covered. Blessed is the man unto whom the LORD imputeth not iniquity." Paul interprets this non-imputation of sin as the positive imputation of the righteousness of Christ (Rom. 4:6). This is the only answer to guilt. When you have Christ, your sins are gone, your guilt is removed, and all accusation is silenced. "Who shall lay any thing to the charge of God's elect? It is God that justifieth. Who is he that condemneth?" (Rom. 8:33, 34). Where is the man—where is the devil—who can condemn a man who has Jesus Christ? Listen! here is God's answer. Christ died. Christ is risen. Christ is even now at the right hand of God. Christ maketh intercession for us. These truths have been well termed "The Four Pillars of the Gospel." Happy are the people of God. They have Christ, and the old accusation of unresolved guilt is silenced for time and eternity.

Moreover, all condemnation is gone forever. "There is therefore now no condemnation to them which are in Christ Jesus" (Rom. 8:1). That is

15

the negative way of stating it. Paul also described it in positive language: "Blessed be the God and Father of our Lord Jesus Christ, who hath blessed us with all spiritual blessings in heavenly places in Christ" (Eph. 1:3). Then follows an amazing list. "He hath chosen us" (v. 4). I can never understand why Christians are so often bitter against the truth of election, that God chose us before the foundation of the world. I can understand the ungodly, for "the natural man receiveth not the things of the Spirit," and he would fain, like Satan, climb to the throne of God and dethrone his Maker. However, I cannot understand a Christian desiring to insist, "No, Lord, You must have made a mistake; it is I who first chose You," or at best, "You chose me only because You foresaw that I would choose You." I would rather rejoice, as the Apostle did, in the free, sovereign, electing purpose of God. Our choice is fickle and so very changeable. There would be little happiness in the thought that our salvation depended on our will power, but God says He has chosen us. What a blessing! Do not try to explain it away, but rejoice in it.

If some believers become upset at the declaration that God chose us, they become positively angry at the next statement in Ephesians 1: He "predestinated us." There is no need for us ever to be worried about that word. The word Paul uses is the one that gives us our English word *horizon*. The Lord preset our limits, as it were. He settled our destiny before time began. Do I understand that? Not at all, I do not understand it. Do I understand the Trinity? No, not at all. Can I explain the virgin birth? No, I cannot. But do I believe them? Do I rejoice in them? Do they bless my soul? Thank God, they do. And so does the glorious truth that He made His people the object of His favour before the beginning of time, graciously giving us to Christ in the covenant of redemption and ensuring that through His merit we would arrive in heaven. He has chosen us. He has predestinated us. Paul goes on to say that He has made us accepted in the beloved; He has redeemed us; He has given us an inheritance (vv. 6-11). What a list of blessings Christians have in Christ! Its message is plain: those who have Christ have everything that pertains to life and godliness—and that means everything that produces true happiness.

But think again. We must see that Christians enjoy more than the mere blessings of Christ. *It is Christ Himself who fully satisfies His people*. Mere things never bless, never satisfy. We see this in the natural realm. Because a man is the richest man in town does not mean he is the happiest man in town. Similarly, the blessings of God (and I say this very reverently) considered in themselves—which is something the Bible never does, though unfortunately men tend to—the blessings of God considered in themselves do not satisfy the soul. It is Christ who satisfies the soul. It is Christ ministering those blessings who satisfies the soul. According to Psalm 68:19, the Lord "daily loadeth us with benefits." Jeremiah said in the midst of a very doleful passage in Lamentations chapter 3 that God's mercies "are new every morning." Thank God for the things which the Lord gives us, but, bless God, it is Christ who satisfies us. Psalm 107 puts it very well: "O give thanks unto the LORD, for he is good: for his mercy endureth for ever. Let the redeemed of the LORD say so, whom he hath redeemed from the hand of the enemy; and gathered them out of the lands, from the east, and from the west, from the north, and from the south. They wandered in the wilderness in a solitary way; they found no city to dwell in. Hungry and thirsty, their soul fainted in them. Then they cried unto the LORD in their trouble, and he delivered them out of their distresses. . . . Oh that men would praise the LORD for his goodness, and for his wonderful works to the children of men!" Do you see the emphasis here? He fills the hungry soul.

He satisfies the longing soul. The soul has four great needs if it is to be satisfied, and the Lord Jesus meets them all. To be satisfied, the soul needs peace. It also needs power. Then it needs to have a real purpose, and finally it needs a prospect. Without those it will never be satisfied. Think of these four needs.

Our soul needs *peace,* such a peace as will enable us to look up into the face of God without fear. Who can give us such a peace? It seems impossible. Yet it is absolutely necessary that a poor worm of the dust, a self-confessed, self-condemned criminal who deserves only to be damned eternally, should be able to look into the face of the Holy One without fear of retribution if he is ever to have peace of soul. Such a thing is beyond our reach by nature, but the gospel is that Jesus Christ has made peace through the blood of His cross. He enables us to look up into the face of God without fear.

We also need a peace that enables us to look back to face our past without shame. I have already talked about the problems of guilt. What can you do about that? The question is rather, "What has Christ done about it?" He has put away sin by the sacrifice of Himself, and therefore the child of God has peace, praising God as did the psalmist in Psalm 103:12: "As far as the east is from the west, so far hath he removed our transgressions from us." Our sins are eternally removed. We can look back to the pit from which we were dug and the rock from which we were hewn. We can look back and face a past that otherwise would haunt us, and we can say, "It is under the blood."

> *My sin—oh the bliss of this glorious thought!—*
> *My sin, not in part but the whole,*
> *Is nailed to His cross, and I bear it no more;*
> *Praise the Lord, praise the Lord, O my soul.*

We need a peace that not only looks up without fear, and looks back without shame, but that can look in to face ourselves without turmoil. As I have talked with people over a period of years, I have found that their biggest problem is in themselves. Many and many a time I have had people come to me and say, "The gospel tells me that God has forgiven me, but how can I forgive myself? I'm ashamed of myself." None of us can examine our own hearts without shame. In and of ourselves there is nothing lovely about us. That is why the New Testament continually reminds God's people that they are in Christ. God views them in Christ. God clothes them with Christ. He directs their attention to their Saviour and to themselves only in their Saviour. That is how to look at yourself. This is not to make light of sin. Far from it, for when you see Christ your heart will be stirred to holiness. Frequently when dealing with Christians who have difficulty progressing beyond looking at themselves with constant loathing I have turned their attention to Numbers chapter 23. Balaam was trying to curse the people of God for money. But he could not do it. Instead he was compelled to confess, "Behold, I have received commandment to bless: and he hath blessed; and I cannot reverse it. He hath not beheld iniquity in Jacob, neither hath he seen perverseness in Israel" (vv. 20-21). Now mark that statement, because Israel was far from perfect, just as far from being perfect as you and I are. Any man looking at them could have found fault and said, "Lord, do You not see this and hear that?" There were things that disrupted their fellowship with God. In

Numbers 23, however, the subject is blessing and cursing, salvation and damnation, and God is saying, "These people are under the blood. These people are covered by the power of the sacrifice. When I look at them, I see no iniquity. I recognize no sin. They cannot be cursed." When you realize the force of the divine argument here, you will know what Paul meant in Hebrews 9:14 when he said that your conscience is purged by the blood of Christ. When you have that purging of conscience you can look in at yourself without self-blame and without the turmoil that otherwise would wreck every vestige of happiness within your soul.

If you are going to have peace, you must also be able to look out and face the world. There is nothing in this world that makes for peace. Nothing. The politics of this world do not make for peace. The economics of this world may apparently, but do not in reality, make for peace. The societal relationships of this world do not make for peace. There is nothing in this world that makes for peace. This is a world that is out to wreck the peace of the children of God. Oh, that God's people would recognize it! Friendship with the world is enmity with God, because the world is against God and His people. We are in the world, but we are not of it. In this world there are tribulations. Maybe you have been through some of those tribulations. At times you have felt you would rather die than live. You would rather give up than go on. The home is under pressure. The business is under pressure. Your mind is under pressure. Your heart is under pressure. Your whole life is under pressure. During all this conflict the devil is absolutely merciless. There is never a hold barred, never a foul trick he will not play. There is no person whose weakness would elicit the slightest feeling of compassion from him. He would delight all the more to wreck him when he is at his weakest. But listen! Jesus said in John 16:33, "In the world ye shall have tribulation: but be of good cheer; I have overcome the world." I love the words of John 14:27: "Peace I leave with you, my peace I give unto you. . . . Let not your heart be troubled, neither let it be afraid." Christians have the promise of peace despite the unquiet world in which they live. Indeed, the peace of God keeps (literally, stands guard over) the heart and mind of all who trust, praise, and pray (Phil. 4:6, 7).

We need a peace that can look up into the face of God. We need a peace that can look back and face our past, that can look in and face ourselves, that can look out and face the world, and that can look forward and face the future. God's people so often are made to worry about what is going to happen. Most of the worries are about things that never happen. We are forever trying to cross bridges before we come to them. In most instances we will never come to them, because they do not exist. If the devil can get us worrying about the future, painting the blackest possible picture for us, he will rob us of our peace. Did not the Lord Jesus Christ say in John 14:1, "Let not your heart be troubled: ye believe in God, believe also in me"? Do you not believe in God? Do you see then what the Saviour is saying? "You believe in God, and you are worried about the future. You believe in God, and you are trembling at the devil's opposition. You believe in Me, and yet you allow Satan and the world to cast doubt and fear into your mind as if the future will see all your joys, all your hopes, and all God's promises unraveling and coming to nothing." Such a thing can never be. Thus He says, "Let not your heart be troubled: ye believe in God, believe also in me." Then He takes you right into the future as if there were nothing between the present moment and heaven. "In my Father's house are many mansions" (v. 2). The meaning is unmistakeable: "Nothing can change the glorious truth that I have a place in heaven for you. Nobody can take that from you." Notice how the Lord Jesus makes this point. He does not mention even one event between the moment of speaking and the moment of our entering into glory. It is just as if He had said that this hiatus between the time we meet the Lord in grace and the time we meet Him face to face can make no change in our certain entrance into glory. Romans chapter 8 spells out the very same truth: "Whom he did foreknow, he also did predestinate to be conformed to the image of his Son. . . . Moreover whom he did predestinate, them he also called: and whom he called, them he also justified." Now see the next step. Had any uninspired man been writing it he would have said, "Whom He justified, them He also sanctified." And that would introduce the whole realm of human experience and the ups and downs of temptations, failures, and restorations. But the Holy Spirit does not mention sanctification here. He says, "Whom he justified, them he also glorified." Why move straight from justification to glorification? Because there is nothing that can undo what God has done to render us accepted in His sight on the merits of Jesus Christ. That is what this text is saying. What peace this gives to face the future! The soul needs peace, and He is our peace.

The soul needs not only peace, but *power*. We need power against Satan, sin, and self. There are real enemies for the Christian to face. There is an unseen world in mortal combat with us. Sometimes, because it is unseen, we tend to forget it is there. I never like jokes about the devil. The devil is no joke, and he is never more dangerous than when he becomes a joke. "We wrestle . . . against principalities, against powers, against the rulers of the darkness of this world, against spiritual wickedness in high places" (Eph. 6:12). What tensions often fill the heart of the child of God! What a spiritual bombardment is loosed against him! He needs victory over Satan. He also needs victory over sin, and the glorious truth is that Christ gives it. "Sin shall not have dominion over you" (Rom. 6:14). This is not a promise to an elite in the church. It is God's statement of fact regarding His justified people, for the rest of the verse reads, "Ye are not under the law, but under grace." In other words, "We are justified; we are dead with Christ; we are risen with Christ; we are one with Christ. Therefore sin will not have dominion over us." Christ gives victory over sin and Satan.

Praise God, He also gives victory over self to serve Him. The apostle Paul could say in Philippians 4:13, "I can do all things through Christ which strengtheneth me." There is power to do the will of God, however great our natural weakness. If the Lord wants you to do anything, be assured you can do it. This is not the so-called power of positive thinking, something that is a mere humanistic delusion, a counterfeit of the real spiritual power the Lord promises to His people. No, this is something much more precious. Whom the Lord calls, He equips and enables. Jesus Christ dwells within His people in the person of His Holy Spirit, enabling them to do all that the will of God entails. He said to His disciples—it is often overlooked that this is the last promise Christ ever gave them before His ascension—"Ye shall receive power, after that the Holy Ghost is come upon you" (Acts 1:8). If there is a missing ingredient among the people of God and in the church of Christ today, it is the power of the Holy Ghost. This is inexcusable, because our risen Lord has made full provision for every one of His people to have the power of His Spirit to serve Him.

The soul needs peace. Christ gives peace. The soul needs power— power over sin, over Satan, and over self, and power to do the will of God. Christ gives that power.

The soul also needs *purpose*. Purposelessness and aimlessness mean misery, despair, and hopelessness. If we could read the heart of every suicide, we would find that a time came when he was utterly convinced that his life was worth nothing and could accomplish nothing. I have spoken to people who have faced this, people who have been on the very edge of self-murder, and their thinking has been, "I can see no reason for me to live." Now the world has an answer to this. It goes something like this: "You are an individual. Assert yourself. Do your own thing. Get liberated. Recognize that you have merely lost your self-esteem. Start trying to like yourself and build up a positive self-image. Or take an interest in some new activity, or make your life count in helping others." Helping others is all very well, but the humanist approach is all so much empty jargon, the product of a depraved mind that wants to substitute its own ideas for God's Word. It may bring some measure of temporary relief, but it will never really help or satisfy the soul. Despite the world's best efforts, for many people life has become a drudgery, with no real purpose and no sign of any real worth. For all such people there is an answer, God's answer. His answer is Christ. Christ satisfies. Do you remember what Paul said in Philippians chapter 1? He said, "To me to live is Christ." When a man can say that, he has the greatest purpose and goal a soul can have. I Corinthians 10:31 tells us, "Whether therefore ye eat, or drink, or whatsoever ye do, do all to the glory of God." A Christ-centred life is the answer to the soul's need of a worthy purpose.

Every Christian can have this purpose, not just the especially gifted or successful ones. All Christians are in Christ; they are all part of His body. Now, there are parts of your body that you may do without, parts that therefore appear relatively unimportant or unnecessary. For instance, you may need to go into hospital and have your appendix removed. In the spiritual realm, however, there is not one part of the body of the Lord that is unnecessary. In His body there are people who are very prominent. They are people who have outstanding God-given abilities, and they are very much needed. But many more have no such apparent usefulness. You may feel that you are one of the ungifted. How often you have lamented, "I can't sing; I can't play piano; I can't speak in public; I can't . . ." The devil loves to make a Christian say, "I can't, I can't, I can't." The devil is a liar. If the Lord wants you to sing, He will give you a voice to sing. He is going to

22

prove that when He brings you to heaven, is He not? The thing you should never forget is that God has placed you in the body. He has made you what you are in the body. Just live for Jesus Christ, and if your life for Christ is hidden completely, as some parts of the human body are, remember that very often the hidden parts of the body are in reality the most important. You may have a ministry in the secret place, laying hold of God to prosper the work of His Son. What could be more important? Whatever place the Lord has given you in His body is worthwhile and will bring everlasting glory to His Name. So do what He gives you to do for His glory. It doesn't matter who you are or what you are—greatly talented or severely limited—if you want to live for Jesus Christ and are willing to say, "Lord, for me to live is Christ," you will have the greatest purpose and fulfilment in life that a man can have. That is why the New Testament addresses parents and children, masters and servants, elders, deacons, and saints. The apostle John spoke to fathers and to young men. It does not matter who you are, what you are, where you are, or whether you are talented or what we call ordinary. Most of us are not very talented. It does not matter what place you occupy in the body; you are a witness and a worker for your Lord, a vital part of God's purpose and God's work. There is never a reason for a Christian to say, "There's no purpose for me."

We need peace, we need purpose, we need power, and we need a prospect. Thank God, there is a goal in view. Christ gives us that. We are pressing "toward the mark for the prize of the high calling of God in Christ Jesus." What a joy to know that heaven is our assured destination! As we journey through this world, we are going home. We are going to see our Saviour. Whether He comes for us in His glorious second advent or calls us to Himself through death, He sets before us the prospect of everlasting bliss. We have a blessed hope that grows brighter every day we live. Christ fully satisfies His people.

The point I am trying to prove is that God's people are truly blessed. Psalm 115:15 says, "Ye are blessed of the LORD which made heaven and earth." I would to God we could say that of every one of us. Alas, I fear that is not possible, because there are some of you who do not know Christ as your Saviour.

The fact that Christ pronounces His people blessed carries grave implications for all who are not His people.

23

No Man Is Truly Happy Who Does Not Know the Lord

He may be rich in land and store. He may be powerful in worldly influence. He may be satiated with worldly pleasure. His ears may be deafened with worldly applause, but if he knows not Christ he cannot be happy, because he is under the curse of God. Think of it. If you are not saved, if you do not have the Lord Jesus Christ as your personal Saviour, then your sins remain unforgiven. Consider every vile and filthy sin of nature and of practice, all the ungodliness of a life that has been lived outside of God's will and in rebellion to God's law, and then remember that every part and particle of it is noted against you in the records of God, undeleted, unforgiven, and unwashed. What on earth can ever remove the foul and filthy stain of sin? If you do not know Christ, there is nothing that can do it. Your conscience must continue its reign as an accuser within your breast. If you are unsaved, the last thing you are really willing to do is sit down and even listen to your own conscience. It is like the candle of the Lord within you that searches the deep hidden places of your soul. It will not allow you to forget about the things you would rather obliterate from your memory. It resurrects thoughts that you buried long ago. It re-enacts scenes that you have sought to erase from your mind. Again and again, with all the force and fury of Mount Sinai, your conscience comes accusing you. You cannot be happy while you have a conscience that accuses you, while you have a mind that is enmity against God, and while the wrath of God abides upon you. You cannot be happy while your hold on this life is so weak and tenuous that there is only one tiny step between your soul and the pit of utter destruction. Happy? Never! It is impossible for an unsaved man to have true blessedness. I know the world has its song, but the song of the world is but the death rattle in the throats of the ungodly. I know the world has its laughter, but I also know that the Holy Spirit has said that the laughter of fools is like the crackling of thorns under the pot. The fire is already burning, and their very laughter is but the evidence of a depraved heart and of the wrath of God against it. Happy? No man can be truly happy or blessed who does not know the Lord. Unsaved men want to be happy, to have their thrills, to "live." How can a man be happy when there is less than a paper wall between his soul and a lost eternity, when the law of God thunders against him and the sword of divine judgment is suspended over his head? How can he be happy when all he can look forward to is the sentence of God to the everlasting fire, turmoil, darkness, and pain of a lost eternity? No man can be happy who is yet a stranger to God and His Christ. God's people are truly blessed. All others are truly cursed. That leads to a final observation.

THE PRESENT STATE IS A FORETASTE OF ETERNITY

Sinners are condemned already (John 3:18). They are now under the wrath and curse of God, but there is a vast difference between being in this state and having the full fury of that wrath actually poured out upon them. It is something like the difference between being on death row and actually suffering capital punishment. Sinners are now judged guilty. The final execution of the sentence upon them is soon to come. When the day of the wrath of the Lamb arrives and sinners call upon the rocks and mountains to fall upon them and hide them (Rev. 6:15-17), every vestige of those things which appear to contradict the Biblical message about the cursed condition of sinners will be stripped away. I have been saying that sinners cannot be happy as long as they are out of Christ and under God's curse. But sinners deceive themselves. At times they argue, "If God is angry with us, why are we so prosperous? If we are under the curse, how is it that we are enjoying life so much? Our pleasure and prosperity strongly contradict your message that we cannot be happy without Christ." Listen! I am talking about reality. Even if you have great possessions, without Christ you are under the curse of God. Soon your possessions will be removed with everything else that appears to bring ease and comfort. Then the soul in all its naked ungodliness will bear the full and eternal fury of the curse of an offended God. Do not be deceived. Your present state is merely a foretaste of eternity.

Similarly, *the present state of Christians is merely a foretaste of an eternity which Jesus describes with the word* heaven. There every vestige of sorrow, pain, and trial will be removed forever. "God himself shall be with them, and be their God. And God shall wipe away all tears from their eyes; and there shall be no more death, neither sorrow, nor crying, neither shall there be any more pain: for the former things are passed away" (Rev. 21:3, 4). It is difficult to remember that when hot tears are staining your face and your heart is breaking under some weighty trial, but soon all your labour and suffering will be over. You will enter into the joy of your Lord and never again experience a pang or a pain of any description. In heaven there will be nothing to mar the bliss of the redeemed. It is good to be saved here and now. Think of all we have in Christ—and this is just the beginning! I have a friend in Belfast who received Christ as his Saviour and was overflowing with the joy of sins forgiven and the prospect of glory to follow. His way of expressing my point was, "Just think of it! All this and heaven to follow!" Now we are redeemed, but we are still in this body of humiliation. This body causes us so much trouble. It is a vehicle of corruption and sin, but, praise the Lord, the day of the redemption of the body is coming. Then it will be freed from all its weakness and be made like unto Christ's glorious body (Phil. 3:21). Now we are children of God and have received the Spirit of adoption, but according to Romans 8:23 that adoption is to be consummated at the redemption of the body. Now we are assured of our eternal inheritance; then we shall be presented publicly and made to enter into it in all its heavenly fulness.

All this is ahead of God's people. Remember where you were when the Lord Jesus found you. You were a poor, wretched, miserable, guilty sinner, within a heartbeat of a lost eternity. Now see where He is going to bring you. He will very soon proclaim you His child before heaven, earth, and hell, and lead you into the fulness of His inheritance among the saints. Now we are united to Christ by faith. What a day it will be when we shall see Him face to face to tell the story, "saved by sovereign grace."

Jesus said, "Blessed are ye"—a present, perfect, irreversible blessing. Put the emphasis on the last word: "Blessed are *ye*." Then ask the question, "Am I blessed of God? Have I Jesus Christ as my Saviour? Does Christ satisfy my soul?" Here I want to be very frank with you. I fear that there are multitudes today who have religion and all the ordinances of the church but who have no heart for Jesus Christ. He is not their joy and satisfaction. They may wrap themselves in the cloak of empty religious profession and comfort themselves that it is well with their souls, but they have a rude awakening awaiting them. However weak a Christian's faith may be, however stumbling his steps, his heart is taken up with Christ.

26

Are you blessed of the Lord? That is a serious question, for if you are not blessed of God you are cursed of God. There are really only two classes of men in the world. There will be only two classes at the judgment. Matthew chapter 25 speaks of the blessed and the cursed. Those are the only two classes of people there are. To which class do you belong? Do you aim for happiness? Do you intend to escape what the Lord Jesus Christ called "the damnation of hell"? Then learn the lesson of our text. Happiness here and hereafter belongs to God's people—and to no one else. Christ is the One you need. He alone can save and satisfy. The gospel is that He will save and satisfy every soul who comes to Him. He invites you. He says, "Come unto me, all ye that labour and are heavy laden, and I will give you rest" (Matt. 11:28). Obey that call and come. It is a tragedy for men and women to hear the gospel and refuse the call of God. They are like the Israelites of whom the Lord spoke in Psalm 81:13, 16: "Oh that my people had hearkened unto me, and Israel had walked in my ways! . . . He should have fed them also with the finest of the wheat: and with honey out of the rock should I have satisfied thee." However, they refused to be satisfied by the Lord, and He issued this terrible sentence: "So I gave them up unto their own hearts' lust" (v. 12). Given up by God! That is the ultimate tragedy. You may be fed and satisfied by Christ, or you may be given up. If you come to Him He says He will save and satisfy your soul. If you do not He will give you up. Which will it be?

I close with the words of Moses: "I call heaven and earth to record this day against you, that I have set before you life and death, blessing and cursing: therefore choose life, that both thou and thy seed may live" (Deut. 30:19). Life and death. Blessing and cursing. Heaven and hell. Choose life. Choose blessing. Choose heaven. Choose Christ.

CHAPTER THREE

The Biography of a Christian

Matthew 5:3-12

What therefore God hath joined together, let not man put asunder" (Matt. 19:6). These familiar words lay down not only the permanence of the marriage relationship, which they obviously do, but the permanence of everything God has joined together. In the Scriptures of truth, the Lord has clearly joined together certain things, and we must never try to put those things asunder.

In Matthew chapter 5 we have a number of things which the Lord Himself has joined together. Many understand each Beatitude to describe a different kind of person. The poor in spirit are seen as different people from those who mourn, who in turn are different from those who are meek, who are different from those who hunger and thirst after righteousness. Thus we place the people described by the Lord into so many exclusive categories. This is clearly a mistake. The Beatitudes portray only one character, and that is the character of people who are truly saved. These saved people are described by a list of graces wrought in their hearts by the Spirit of God. That leads me to make this far-reaching statement: You cannot have one of these graces without having the rest. You cannot be saved without having all of the things which the Lord Jesus here enumerates, at least in some measure.

If you study this list of graces very carefully you will discover that there is a glorious progression from a state of spiritual destitution to the reception of glorious rewards in heaven. What we have then in the Beatitudes is **the spiritual biography of the child of God**— the story of the workings of God's grace as He takes a man from that place where He finds him in all his sin and shame, saves him, and keeps on working with him, bringing him finally to heaven and planting him there in the midst of everlasting glory.

Emptied of All Hope in the Flesh

The story commences with the poor in spirit (v. 3). "Blessed are the poor in spirit." The word translated "poor" signifies utter and complete poverty. The picture is of a person destitute of all spiritual esteem for himself and emptied of all spiritual hope in himself. This is the very first mark—the first stirring— of grace in the life of a man whom the Lord ultimately brings to heaven. God first of all moves upon a man's soul to bring him to the end of himself. This is not only the first but very often the most difficult step in our spiritual experience. Proud flesh rebels against it. The Lord Jesus started this sermon on this note for a very good reason. He was, after all, preaching to Jews, and the Jews were notorious for their pride in their religion and in their nation, in their law and in all its ceremonies. Ultimately, theirs was pride in their own works of self-righteousness. The Jews were puffed up with ideas of their own spiritual worthiness, and so before He could give the gospel to them, the Lord Jesus set out to puncture their pride. He said in effect, "You must first of all learn that the blessing of the gospel can come only to those who are poor in spirit, to those who have been divested of every hope in themselves, who have been emptied of all self-confidence and all self-satisfaction in their own self-righteousness."

The Saviour frequently was at pains to press home this point. In Luke chapter 18 we read His story of two men who went up into the temple to pray, the one a Pharisee, the other a publican. The Pharisee "stood and prayed thus with himself"—a very, very telling statement. He prayed with himself, for Almighty God was not listening. Nor was He pleased. The offering of the wicked, including their prayer, is an abomination unto God (Prov. 28:9). So this poor, bloated, self-righteous Pharisee "prayed thus with himself," and he said, "God, I thank thee, that I am not as other men are." Can you imagine the arrogance of a creature who would come into the presence of his Creator and say, "I thank Thee"—not for what God is, not for what God has done, not for what God has spoken, not for the revelation of grace, but—"I thank Thee that I am not a sinner as other men are"? When a person gets to that stage he certainly needs to have his pride punctured. And so, dealing with people of that mentality, the Lord Jesus started His spiritual biography of a child of God with this truth: grace begins its saving work by emptying a person of every notion of self-righteousness.

The testimony of the apostle Paul emphasized the same truth. He had been a Pharisee and had been just as proud as any other Pharisee of his self-righteousness. He said, indeed, that according to the standard of righteousness accepted among the Pharisees he had been more righteous than others. He had more cause to boast than others, but his testimony as a Christian was, "What things were gain to me, those I counted loss for Christ. Yea, doubtless, and I count all things but loss"—the "all things" of legal obedience, of the Jewish religion, the things in which he as a Pharisee had taken such pride—"I count all things but loss for the excellency of the knowledge of Christ Jesus my Lord" (Phil. 3:7, 8). What he was saying was that no man can know the Lord until he has suffered this loss of self-righteousness, self-satisfaction, and self-esteem. That is why in verse 3 of the same chapter he spoke of God's people as those who "worship God in the spirit, and rejoice in Christ Jesus, and have no confidence in the flesh."

This is where the work of grace commences, emptying a man of all reliance on himself and showing him the poverty and the need of his soul. Only when a man has seen that he is destitute will he look for the riches of God's grace in the Lord Jesus Christ and honestly desire Him as Lord and Saviour.

FEELING THE PLAGUE OF SIN

When a man desires Christ, when he sees his emptiness, he will feel his awful plague of sin, and when he feels the plague of sin he will mourn. Matthew 5:4 says, "Blessed are they that mourn." When a sinner has been emptied of self and has seen the utter uselessness of the works of the flesh, he will be brought to see the deep pit of his own sinfulness and depravity. He will mourn his guilt, his past wickedness, and his present corruption of nature. His life will be a grief unto him. This mourning indeed may even

31

tempt him to despair. When a man really comes under conviction of sin, there is very often a period when he throws up his hands and wonders if there could possibly be any hope for such as he. In their evangelism the Puritans liked to emphasize what they called "law work." Some preachers may have gone too far in that direction, but I cannot help but think that nowadays there is such an emphasis on inflating statistics by registering innumerable decisions that there are people being led to professions who have never mourned their sin. Jesus said, "Blessed are they that mourn." Anything in our evangelism that makes light of the tears and mourning for sin of a sinner seeking Christ is foolish and wrong. I know that a sinner is not saved by tears, and I would agree with Henry Moorehouse when he said that he would not put even a tear between a sinner and his Saviour. I quite agree with that. I would not put anything between a sinner and the Saviour. Nor did the Lord put even a tear between the sinner and Himself. What He said was simply that when the Word of God is preached and understood, sinners will not only see their emptiness but will come to view sin as they have not viewed it before and will mourn over it.

As I said, under the burden of that conviction they may feel so unworthy that all hope will apparently flee. But, praise God, the gospel has a message of hope and comfort for souls who are feeling the guilt of sin. I want to emphasize this to you who already have professed faith in Christ. I have discovered that behind many a smiling face, very often behind a Christian testimony, there is a heart that is torn asunder by the grief of guilt—a soul that is struggling with the awful turmoil caused by the guilt of past sin and the feeling of shame and guilt caused by an inward, corrupted nature. To make matters worse, as the feeling of guilt and shame continues despite the most rigourous religious observance, a question begins to haunt the soul: "Is this from God, or is it from the devil? Is this a message from God to save me, or is it a message from the devil to confuse me?" This naturally leads to the soul-searching inquiry, "Am I really saved? Has my guilt ever been dealt with? Did I ever really repent and believe the gospel?" My friend, my message to you is that the gospel has a word of comfort for the guilty. You can always discern the subtle attack of Satan from the conviction of the Lord. Satan always seeks to turn your eye away from Christ and to dissuade your heart from trusting Christ. He will try to frustrate you by having you dissect your act of faith in first coming to Christ. He will ensure that he keeps you confused about how you really felt and how sincere you really were. As long as he succeeds in such ruses, he will rob you of arriving at the peace of the gospel. Here is a word of advice. The New Testament never focuses on saving faith as something in the past tense. The question is not, *"Did* I believe in Christ?" but *"Do* I believe in Christ?" God's people are those who are the constantly believing ones. This then is the question, and it drives us away from a futile attempt to recapture the emotions of a distant moment in the past to a consideration of Christ, His gospel, and His promise. If you want your guilt dealt with, bring it to Christ and have it dealt with in the light of the gospel. Remember this simple truth, especially you who are tormented by guilt and find it difficult to discern whether you are enduring an attack of the devil or are under the conviction of the Holy Spirit: Satan will cause you to grieve so as to keep you away from Christ, but the Holy Spirit will convict you to lead you to trust Christ and enter into peace through Him.

Only a mourning that leads to Christ is wrought of God. A man needs to feel the guilt of his sin. He needs to feel that he is by nature a brand who deserves to be burned in the fire of hell. He needs to know that the guilt of his sin is in one way like a mountain, and in another like a deep pit. He needs to know that he has offended God and that God could justly damn him to the deepest hell. Oh, a sinner needs to feel the guilt of his sin, but, bless God, the more acute the sense of guilt, the more glorious the sense of release. The gospel message is clear and simple and plain. It is powerful and glorious. The message of the gospel, in the words of Isaiah 1:18, is, "Though your sins be as scarlet, they shall be as white as snow." The message as the apostle John gave it is, "The blood of Jesus Christ his Son cleanseth us from all sin. . . . If we confess our sins, he is faithful and just to forgive us our sins, and to cleanse us from all unrighteousness." (I John 1:7, 9). There has never been any advance on the message that John the Baptist preached at Bethabara beyond Jordan, when he turned the gaze of guilty sinners to Christ and cried, "Behold the Lamb of God, which taketh away the sin of the world" (John 1:29). Bless God, there is an answer to guilt. The message of the gospel is that there is power in the blood of Jesus Christ to destroy and remove forever every last vestige of the guilt of sin.

33

A WILLING ACCEPTANCE OF GOD'S WAY OF SAVING SINNERS

King Solomon said in Proverbs 25:25, "As cold waters to a thirsty soul, so is good news from a far country." The comfort of the gospel is good news to a guilty sinner mourning his sin in the far country, cut off from God. When that good news comes to him like water to a thirsty soul in the desert, he gladly accepts it. That is why in verse 5 of Matthew 5 the Lord Jesus says, "Blessed are the meek."

Meek is a very interesting word. Archbishop Trench rightly noted in his work on New Testament synonyms that the word here does not basically describe a person's outward behaviour. It does not describe his relations with other men. It does not even describe his natural disposition. Rather— and this is important—it denotes a willing acceptance of God's dealing with him. That is what it is to be meek: to have a willing acceptance of God's dealings with us.

You will notice how accurate the Scripture is in employing this word just here. It is giving the spiritual biography of the child of God, and the picture is absolutely true to life. The sinner first of all sees himself as empty. He mourns over his sin. He hears the good news from the far country, and then he totally accepts God's Word and God's terms. That is how you are saved. "This is a faithful saying, and worthy of all acceptation, that Christ Jesus came into the world to save sinners" (I Tim. 1:15). You have no doubt heard many a learned disquisition on what it is to believe, what it is to have faith. What is faith? Some of the definitions of "simple faith" which foolish theologians have given are meaningless jumbles of words. Søren Kierkegaard, the father of existential theology, is a perfect example: "Faith is, that the self, in relation to itself, will be itself and then, transparent to itself, bases itself in the Power (that is, in God) who posits the Self." Are you not glad the Lord did not leave our souls to the tender mercies of such philosophers? Thankfully not all theologians have been so unscriptural. An old Scottish theologian, Thomas Halyburton, saw right to the heart of the matter and summed it all up very nicely and very briefly: faith is simply a sinner's hearty acceptance of God's way of saving souls. The more you think of this the more you will appreciate the genius of the man and the statement. What is it to be meek? What is it to accept Jesus

Christ? What is it to exercise faith? Here is the answer: You are at the end of yourself, with no hope in your own works or your own righteousness. You are grieving over the guilt of your sin. You hear the message of the gospel. The gospel says that it is not by the works of righteousness that you have done, but by God's mercy that you are saved. It is by grace alone. It is on the merit of the blood of Christ alone. Faith whole-heartedly accepts that divine way of salvation and asks for none other.

Generally, people hate this word about the blood. For centuries men have been trying to erase the blood from the Bible message. They will make the blood mean anything but blood. Our old, vicious, carnal nature does not mind speaking about the life of Jesus, or even the death of Jesus, but it detests all mention of the blood of Jesus. But the blood is God's way of saving souls. He recognizes no other way. There is not a soul saved from hell except by the blood of Christ. There is not a soul in heaven except by the merit of that blood. In heaven they sing about the blood. It is a tragedy that in so many hymn books there is a scarcity of hymns about the blood. It is difficult to find good hymns about the blood. Sweet-sounding poetry about mountains and valleys and rivers and such things are more acceptable to carnal ears than any reference to the precious blood that purchased our redemption. I have no objection to singing the praise of God for His marvellous creation, but never let even that take the place of the theme of redemption by blood. You can go to hell with hymns of mountains and valleys and rivers. Your poetry will not make hell any less hot. It is the blood that makes atonement for the soul. Yet we try to worship God and sing His praise and preach His gospel apart from the blood. God's way of saving sinners is solely through the merit of Christ's atoning blood. When a man has faith, while he does not understand everything in the scheme of redemption, his heart opens up to God as a flower opens up to the sun. He accepts God's way of saving sinners. He says,

> *I need no other argument,*
> *I need no other plea;*
> *It is enough that Jesus died,*
> *And that He died for me.*

So he fully, whole-heartedly accepts God's gospel in Jesus Christ.

LONGING FOR A TRUE GROUND OF ASSURANCE

Now every soul—and I know this will touch a point that troubles many Christians—every soul on coming to Christ longs to be assured of the ground of his acceptance before God. Thus it is important to note the next stage in the believer's spiritual biography. The Lord Jesus went on to say, "Blessed are they which do hunger and thirst after righteousness."

The soul knows, you would say almost by intuition, that God can accept nothing less than perfection. Therefore the great question is, "How can I be sure I am saved? Yes, I have come to Christ. The preacher preached to me that if I came to Christ I would receive forgiveness. I have come to Christ. But, oh, how can I know? How can I be sure that I am accepted before God?" I am not now describing a false professor, but a soul who has sincerely sought Christ for salvation. Some preachers would lead you to believe that if there is any searching of heart after you have come to Christ, you are not really saved at all. Those preachers do not know their Bible. Hungering and thirsting is a spiritual grace, and when a man has come to Christ and has heartily accepted Him as He is freely offered in the gospel, he longs for a solid ground of assurance. When a man is really hungry, nothing can satisfy him but real food. You may set a lovely bouquet of flowers in front of a ravenously hungry man, but he will not be at all interested. You may play him the most beautiful music; it will mean nothing to him. You may even talk to him about feasts, but that will only make matters worse. When he is hungry, what does he want? He wants food. There are Christians who are longing to know the ground of their assurance and acceptance with God, and all they are receiving is tantamount to a spiritual bunch of flowers or a melodious jingle. All the time their souls are longing to know, "What does God say? Have I any solid ground of being absolutely sure of my soul's salvation?" The answer to their yearning is to see the merit of Christ that is put to their account before God and then to grasp the plain promise of God that He has actually done this gracious work of imputation.

I have dealt with many Christians troubled on this issue of assurance. I recently spoke to one man who presented a sorry spectacle. He said, "I have been to sixty different preachers, and I have made sixty different decisions." But he could not say he was saved. All

36

too often when souls are troubled about assurance, preachers will have them try to remember their decision and examine it for marks of honesty and sincerity. People who are battling doubt will usually confess that they wonder if they were sufficiently sincere or penitent or believing. When they are told that then they should make another decision to accept Christ, they do so only to find a little later that the same process of doubt and fear is recommenced. What they need to be told is that there is no saving merit even in their act of coming to Christ. The merit is in the Christ to whom they come. There is a world of difference. Nothing we do is perfect, and that includes our exercise of faith. If God demands perfection as the ground of our acceptance, it is clear that that ground cannot be in our faith or our decision. It must be in Christ. A believer can be satisfied and assured only when he knows that he possesses the perfect righteousness of Christ in the sight of God. Remember the story of Martin Luther. He almost went insane in the cloisters of an Augustinian monastery as he searched for peace with God. He needed to be saved from wrath, and he knew it. But what did God want of Luther? Did He want him to suffer? Then he would lie in the cold, damp cell all night without heat or warm clothing. He would gladly suffer. Did God want Luther's blood? Then he would lash himself until his body was a gory mess. Did He want Luther's life? Then Luther would starve himself to death. There he was, a young man emaciated, scarred, and dreadfully in need of knowing God's answer to his constant question: "How can I be sure my sins have been forgiven?" Some people doubt the story of how he received God's answer as recorded by a great historian of the Reformation, but it appears to me to be authentic. When Luther was going on hands and knees up the so-called holy staircase in Rome, kissing every step, God flashed that message before his mind and thundered it in his heart: "The just shall live by faith." Paul said that we are justified by faith. On what ground? On the ground of the obedience of Christ (Rom. 5:18-19). On that ground Martin Luther entered into the assurance of eternal life through Christ. That is still the ground of assurance for every doubting soul.

Paul puts it in the plainest possible terms in II Corinthians 5:21. Perhaps you say, "Preacher, I have come to Christ, but there are times when I don't have assurance. The words of F. A. Blackmer's hymn describe me perfectly:

> *Sometimes trusting, sometimes doubting,*
> *Sometimes joyful, sometimes sad.*

At times I am on the mountain top, rejoicing in the Lord. How can I know with an abiding assurance that I am accepted?" The answer of this verse may sound revolutionary to some of you, but it is imperative that this point be fully appreciated. God did not accept you because you made a decision for Christ. God did not accept you because of the prayer you prayed or because of the tears you shed. Has not the devil come along and said, "Were you really sincere enough? Did you really pray the right prayer? Did you have enough feeling?" Have you not been over that ground again and again? Have you not felt the frustration of trying to re-enact or relive that moment that occurred one year ago or twenty years ago when you came to Jesus Christ? You must learn this vital lesson: however precious the memory of turning to Christ is for a Christian, you can never re-feel and relive that moment, and you can never make your assurance depend on a mere memory. You are not accepted because of how you felt, what you felt, or what you said when you came to Christ—however important those things may be, and I have shown the importance of some of them already. You are accepted on the ground of the merits of Christ. What happens when a man comes to Christ? Notice the terms of this great text in II Corinthians 5:21: "He hath made him to be sin for us, who knew no sin; that we might be made the righteousness of God in him." Hugh Martin, a great Scottish preacher and theologian, beautifully paraphrased Paul's words to set forth their full meaning: "God made Him, who knew no sin, to be made sin for us, who knew no righteousness, that we might be made the righteousness of God in Him." What is a Christian's hope for heaven? Think very carefully. It is not, "Lord, I prayed the sinner's prayer," or "I shed bitter tears when I cried to Thee to save me." Praise God, we did cry to Him with a sincere desire for salvation, but that is not our hope for heaven. No! Our hope for heaven is Christ, because He has been made righteousness unto every believer. We have an absolutely perfect righteousness to commend us to God. It is Christ's righteousness. God will accept nothing less and expects nothing more. Paul says that

Christ is made righteousness unto us (I Cor. 1:30). Ah, my friend, God must have perfection as the ground of our acceptance. Well, then, He has all the perfection He desires, for He has Christ. We have all the perfection He desires, for we have Christ, and in the courthouse of God there is not the slightest accusation that can stand against a believing soul, for Jesus Christ is our righteousness. Could you ever ask for a clearer or better ground of acceptance with God? Your spiritual quest for assurance and peace will be realized as you look, not at the greatness of your faith, but at the greatness of Him in whom that faith reposes.

This then is the believer's biography. Feeling his need, emptied of self, mourning his sin, hearing the gospel, accepting Christ, and then realizing that when he comes to Christ he does not merely receive a gift from Christ, he receives Christ Himself. And that is the ground of his assurance. When the doctrine of justification by grace through faith in the merits of Christ—the truth of the imputation of the righteousness of Christ—really grips your heart, life will take on a new dimension of Christian confidence and liberty. I think that is what the hymn writer had in mind when he said,

> *Heaven above is softer blue,*
> *Earth around in sweeter green!*
> *Something lives in every hue*
> *Christless eyes have never seen.*

A Christian Attitude Toward Sinners

When you see Christ as your only hope for heaven you see all that matters. Your soul will be well grounded. You will know that you have been genuinely saved. And the soul that is saved and assured of it cannot hide it. That is something that cannot be bottled up. It must burst forth. When the Lord Jesus went into the house in the area of Tyre and Sidon, "he could not be hid." Is that not a lovely statement? "He could not be hid." If you have Christ in your heart, He cannot be hid. I have often been asked, "What do you think of being a secret disciple?" My answer is that if you want your discipleship to remain a secret you do not know much of the Lord and the joyous power and reality of His presence. Even when

Christians are not able to say much, they surely must display some of the beauty of their Lord. An assurance of salvation always bursts forth. "Blessed are the merciful." Here is an inevitable fruit of a genuine work of grace. As soon as a man is saved he is marked by compassion. The word *mercy* speaks of goodness exercised toward the wretched condition of other people, and a Christian cannot remain unmoved at the wretched condition of men around him. He must be a man of compassion, and that is going to be expressed especially, though not exclusively, in one area. Paul noted this special area of Christian compassion in Romans 11:31 in speaking to the Gentiles regarding the Jews: "Even so have these also now not believed, that through your mercy they also may obtain mercy." What is he saying? Simply that the Jews will be reached for Christ when you have mercy on them and you go out to win them for Him. "Blessed are the merciful." That is speaking of people who have such an experience of God and His grace in Christ that it is bursting out of them so that they have a love for souls, a compassion on the lost, and an interest and involvement in winning the lost for Jesus Christ. That interest and involvement in reaching souls does not belong to only a few in the church. It is the mark of every Christian. I want to be absolutely honest with you. If you can think of souls without Christ and are unmoved to pray or to do anything to see them saved, you have a hard heart toward them. If the sight of your family going down the broad road to hell means nothing to you, or the thought of the world on its way to a lost eternity leaves you cold without a heart compassion for sinners, you need to ask yourself if you have ever known the Lord. "Blessed are the merciful."

A CHRISTIAN ATTITUDE TOWARD THE WORLD

If a Christian is going to do a work for God, he must be personally holy. Thus Jesus says, "Blessed are the pure in heart." You cannot work for God to win souls in this world while you yourself are living in sin. A young woman was drinking in a public bar when a young man came up to her with a drink in his hand and started to talk to her about the Lord. She stopped him dead and told him what kind of a hypocrite she took him to be. She said, "I know I'm a sinner. I know I'm not a Christian. But I know the way of salvation, and I know that no Christian would be standing here drinking with me and then trying to tell me how to be saved. The two things don't go together." I think she seemed to have a better grasp of the truth than he had. If you are going to do anything to reach souls, you yourself must have a clean testimony—not only a good reputation among men, but a good testimony with God. "Blessed are the pure in heart." To be pure in heart is to be separated unto the Lord in heart. God does not justify a man without sanctifying him. He does not give a man salvation without making him habitually holy. I would to God we could say that in this life we were sinless. We are not, but we certainly desire that sinlessness. Robert Murray M'Cheyne said, "Christ for us is all our righteousness before a holy God; Christ in us is all our strength in an unholy world." Here is the great mark of a child of God in this evil world: because of Christ in him, his heart is changed and he is enabled to walk and work *in* the world without being *of* the world. If we are going to serve God, we must be separated from sin.

A Christian Attitude Toward the Saints

It is interesting that in verse 7 of Matthew 5 Christ speaks of the Christian's attitude toward souls: he is merciful. In verse 8 He speaks of the Christian's attitude toward sin: he is pure in heart. We may well say that then in verse 9 He speaks of the Christian's attitude toward the saints: he is a peacemaker. "Blessed are the peacemakers." As we will see in our detailed study of this verse, there is a primary reference to bringing sinners the good news of peace with God through the blood of Christ. However, Paul exhorted believers as well, "Be ye reconciled to God" (II Cor. 5:20). The message of peace and pardon through the blood of Christ should always be kept before God's people. We can do no greater service to the saints than to point them constantly to Christ's satisfaction of God on their behalf. We will encourage and edify the saints if we set out to be Christ's ambassadors to them—constant pointers to the cross. "Be ye reconciled to God"—live constantly in the assurance of peace with God; enjoy daily fellowship with Him and let His peace fill your heart.

When Christians live in the enjoyment of such a fellowship of peace with God they will reflect it in their dealings with their fellow believers. It says much about the virtual ignorance of this fellowship of peace on the part of most professing Christians that our churches are all too often like battlefields. Ephesians 4:3 commands us to endeavour "to keep the unity of the Spirit in the bond of peace." If God's people are not living at peace with each other, they cannot enjoy the unity of the Spirit. They cannot minister Christ one to another. They cannot have a daily enjoyment of the power of the blood. And, of course, they cannot be the powerful witnesses of the gospel of peace that they ought to be to a dying world. That is why the devil works so hard to wreck the peace of the church and set brother against brother. In the church there is nothing more precious than peace among believers, so long as it is not purchased at the expense of God's truth. If ever there should be a dispute or a division in the church, settle it in your heart before God that whoever else may be the devil's tool, it will not be you. Where saints walk in purity and maintain peace among themselves they will assuredly enjoy the Lord's blessing. "Blessed are the peacemakers." That is to be our attitude toward the saints, for as Paul said, "We are called to peace."

The Accuser Overcome

The devil will not take kindly to such a life lived for Christ. In fact, he will roar out his fury. Thus the Saviour said, "Blessed are they which are persecuted for righteousness' sake.... Blessed are ye, when men shall revile you, and persecute you, and shall say all manner of evil against you falsely, for my sake" (Matt. 5:10, 11). False accusation is a wicked part of Satan's persecution and is often more difficult to bear than physical suffering. By persecution and slander the devil seeks to intimidate us, to shame us into silence, and even to lead us into compromise with sin. But our Saviour has made a way of victory for us. "They overcame him [Satan] by the blood of the Lamb, and by the word of their testimony; and they loved not their lives unto the death" (Rev. 12:11). Enjoyment of this overcoming power is the immediate blessing Christians experience when opposed by the devil. Far from persecution and slander causing us to lose our joy and our testimony, they should be taken as an opportunity to prove the Lord and experience His enabling power all the more.

GOD'S IRREVERSIBLE BLESSING

Despite all the opposition of the devil, according to the promise of the Lord Jesus, the believer is blessed. When Baalam looked at Israel with a desire to curse them, he had to confess, "He [the Lord] hath blessed; and I cannot reverse it" (Num. 23:20). Is that not wonderful? The Lord says to every Christian, "I have blessed you," and the devil has to admit, "I cannot reverse it." This is the devil's final concession of defeat. In effect he is forced to cry, "God has blessed that man. I thought I had him. I had chains binding him, but grace snapped the fetters. I had him embroiled in schemes to bring him down to the pit, but the light of God dawned on his soul, and God saved him and cleansed him. I have opposed him and slandered him, but God has blessed him, and I cannot reverse it." Wonderful, wonderful testimony!

IS THIS YOUR TESTIMONY?

This then is the testimony of every child of God. Let me ask you, is this your life story? Have I been describing your testimony? There is nothing on earth as important or valuable as having this personal testimony to the saving, satisfying grace of God in Christ. A saved soul is worth more than all the world. In Mark 8:36 the Lord Jesus made it clear that even if a man could gain the whole world, but lost his soul, he would be a loser forever. So, Christian, rejoice that your name is written in heaven—that, whatever else you have or do not have, you have a saving knowledge of the Lord Jesus Christ.

Could it be that some of you have no such spiritual biography as the one we have just traced? That in fact your story is the very opposite of the one we have been considering? That you are still self-centred, self-righteous, self-complacent, self-satisfied? That while Christ speaks of mourning over sin, you are indulging your sin, loving your sin? Could it be that you have no part in the gospel of the Lord Jesus Christ? That, far from accepting God's way of saving sinners, you have rejected the blood of the Lamb and are yet unblessed and under the curse of God? How can you lay your head upon your pillow at night knowing that you are under the curse of God? In tracing the spiritual biography of the child of God I

43

have shown you the way of salvation, the way of blessing. Confess your need, embrace God's grace in Christ, accept Christ as He is freely offered to you in the gospel, and you will infallibly be saved for all eternity. He has given His word that you will be blessed. His promise is your guarantee, for He cannot and will not go back on His word. He was "delivered for [because of] our offences, and was raised again for [because of] our justification. Therefore being justified by faith, we have peace with God through our Lord Jesus Christ" (Rom. 4:25-5:1). You need none but Christ to save and satisfy for time and eternity. Receive Him today by faith, without seeking to drum up any pretended human merit, and He will give you the spiritual biography that belongs to every child of God.

CHAPTER FOUR

Blessed Poverty!

Blessed are the poor in spirit: for theirs is the kingdom of heaven.
Matthew 5:3

Man's extremity is God's opportunity. So goes the old saying, and while it may be misused and lead to a false theology, it is certainly true that the Lord always brings a man to an end of himself before applying to him the saving balm and benefits of the gospel. Thomas Watson rightly observed, "There is not a more dangerous precipice than self-righteousness." Thus it is the work of God the Holy Spirit to destroy every false hope in a sinner and, having done so, to point him to the Lord Jesus Christ. When He has made him feel his need, He shows him the One who can meet it. When the Lord Jesus promised to send the Holy Spirit into the world, He said, "When he is come, he will reprove the world of sin, and of righteousness, and of judgment" (John 16:8). Until a man is so convinced by the Spirit of God and brought to an end of all hope in himself and in the works of the flesh, he will not receive Christ. His own proud and evil heart will stand in the way. However, when by the grace of God a sinner feels his utter worthlessness and sinfulness, he can come with confidence to Christ, crying to Him with the total assurance that the Saviour will hear, answer, and save him. The Lord Jesus Christ makes this very clear in the first of these Beatitudes in Matthew 5:3: "Blessed are the poor in spirit: for theirs is the kingdom of heaven." We are going to consider **the poor in spirit and the blessing they receive.**

THE MEANING OF "POOR IN SPIRIT"

Right at the beginning it will do us good to understand the meaning of the phrase "the poor in spirit." When the Holy Spirit recorded this statement He chose a word with a very powerful meaning. There were two possible words that Matthew could have used to convey the idea of someone poor. There is a word in II Corinthians 9:9, translated "poor" in our English version, that means simply "one who is so poor that he must earn his daily bread by dint of his own labours." That word could be used of most of us. It is interesting, by the way, to note how words change. The equivalent word in Latin is the word that gives us our word *pauper*. So a pauper actually is simply someone who has to work in order to have enough to live on. He is not one of the idle rich. That is one possible word for "poor" that was available to the inspired penman. The fact that he did not use it should remove every notion that a sinner has anything at all to contribute towards his own salvation. The word Matthew used is a totally different one that means "one who is utterly and completely destitute"— one who lives not by his labour and industry, but by the free gifts of other people. In Luke 16:20, in the story of the rich man and Lazarus, there is a statement that describes Lazarus as a "beggar" who sat at the gate of the rich man day by day. The word *beggar* is exactly the word that is translated "poor" in our text.

I hope you get the picture. The Lord Jesus Christ does not merely portray a man who has a lack. He is not describing a person who is able to do something for himself but who still needs a helping hand from God. The picture given by the Lord Jesus here is of someone in abject and utter destitution who casts himself at the feet of the Lord and on His mercy. I use this expression advisedly, for while the word means "poor," or "a beggar," its verbal form means "to crouch" or "to cringe" before someone. This then is what the Lord Jesus is describing: a poor, destitute sinner who has absolutely nothing he can present to God as even a part payment for His favour but who throws himself before the Lord and cries out for the free gift of grace and mercy. When a man has been brought to see in this inspired Book something of the character of the thrice-holy God, when he has been brought to feel the application of the law of God and know that in himself he is utterly destitute of righteousness and is therefore justly condemned by that law, when he is made to feel his own state as a sinner rightly condemned in God's sight, and when he is then told of God's way of salvation through the substitutionary work of the Lord Jesus Christ, his pride is utterly crushed. He sees himself as vile and inexcusable, rightly condemned, and he confesses with Peter, "I am a sinful man, O Lord." He cries out with Job, "I abhor myself." And thus brought to a sense of his own sin, he sees no goodness in himself but directs his gaze Christ-ward and cries to God for mercy solely on the merits of Christ.

The Saviour told of a Pharisee and a publican who went up to the temple to pray. In Luke 18:13 we read, "The publican, standing afar off, would not lift up so much as his eyes unto heaven, but smote upon his breast, saying, God be merciful to me a sinner." "Be merciful"—those are some of the most important words a sinner can utter. He needs to understand them. They are an appeal for mercy on the ground of the blood atonement. They literally mean, "Lord, be propitiated." A sinner making this appeal to God says in effect, "Lord, look upon the blood of the Lamb. Deal with me on the ground of Calvary. I confess myself to be abjectly devoid of all merit that could commend me to God. I confess myself to be poor and rotten and wicked, fit only to be cast out. But, O Lord, look to Christ. Look to the merit of His precious blood. Look to His sacrifice and wash me in the blood of the Lamb. Give me grace on the ground of Calvary." That is the perfect picture of the man who is poor in spirit. That is the meaning of the term.

THE MARKS OF THE POOR IN SPIRIT

Having come to some understanding of what the Lord Jesus means here, we are now in the position to take another step forward and to consider the marks of the poor in spirit. What does it mean in real-life experience to be poor in spirit? It is one thing to know the meaning of the words; it is another thing to be able to trace the marks of this virtue in our own hearts and lives.

Given the truth of what has already been said, you will notice immediately that the very first mark of the poor in spirit is that *he takes Christ on His own terms.* He has come to an end of argument with God. He has come to an end of parading his self-righteousness. Christ is presented to him in all the sufficiency of His blood atonement, and this man who is poor in spirit takes Him as He is freely offered to him in the gospel and on the terms on which He is offered. In Acts 9:6 we read that as soon as the Lord had unhorsed Saul of Tarsus, that proud Pharisee, and had levelled him to the dust before Him, Saul cried, "Lord, what wilt thou have me to do?" There is a wealth of insight into the change that took place in that man in those words. No longer was Saul a proud Pharisee demanding that God accept him on the ground of his own obedience. No, he was a poor sinner in the dust before God, and he cried to Jesus Christ, "Lord, what do You want me to do? I will take You on Your terms. I will follow You upon Your word." The argument had come to an end. This is the very first mark of the man who is poor in spirit: he has come to Christ and has received Him on the terms on which He is offered in the gospel. I have difficulties with people who say they want to be saved, but on their own terms. I know that not every preacher will agree with me. There are preachers who believe in registering "decisions" at any cost. At times it does not appear to matter how worthless they are, just as long as the magic formula is said. I take leave to disagree. I believe we should exhort sinners to come and receive Christ by faith, but when they profess to take Christ it must be on His terms. Any other "decision" has nothing of the character of saving faith as it is set forth in Scripture. I have had people come to the enquiry room, and I have dealt with them for a long time over the Word of God. They have said, "I want to be saved, but—" The "but" has very often meant, "I would like to know that I am saved from hell, but at the same time I want to hold on to this sin or that sin. I want Christ to save me, but not from this pet sin." The psalmist says, "If I regard iniquity in my heart, the Lord will not hear me" (Psa. 66:18). So there is no point in my going through the charade of an empty decision with someone who is not willing to repent of sin. I have allowed such people to leave without any professed decision for Christ. I have prayed for them, but with no assurance that they have been saved—in fact with a strong conviction that they have not been saved. Sometimes they have left with convulsive weeping, but still unwilling to have Christ save them from their pet sin. Many preachers would tell them to make a decision anyhow and leave the issue of their pet sin to be resolved later. I do not believe that is Biblical or beneficial to the person involved. If a man is actually refusing to have Christ save him from his sin, it is better that he should be faced with the reality of his wickedness and not made to believe that he is receiving Christ by faith. Such a man has not been brought to the place of poverty of spirit where he is willing to take Christ on His terms and not on his own terms. He has not even taken the first step of faith in Christ. According to the Saviour Himself, this poverty of spirit is the first mark of the one who receives His blessing.

Following on from this, you will note that *the one who is poor in spirit will always be an exalter of free grace*. This man will never again speak of his own merit. He will never again boast of his works, or his baptism, or his church, or anything else he is or has done. His whole song will be of grace. When you read the writings of the apostle Paul, mark the emphasis he places on grace. Note some of the tremendous statements he makes about grace. When he was writing to Timothy he said, "The grace of our Lord was exceeding abundant" (I Tim. 1:14). That is a wonderful statement. When he wrote to the church at Ephesus, his sermon and his song were continually of grace—grace from start to finish. How do you know a man is poor in spirit? He has no hope, no confidence in anything but the free grace of God.

I think the supreme mark of the man who is poor in spirit is that *he will always be an exalter of Jesus Christ*. The man who is genuinely poor in spirit understands that only on the merits of Christ is he accepted. It is only because those merits have prevailed with God that this poor sinner is accepted in God's sight. We are poor and destitute in ourselves, but Colossians 2:9, 10, says, "In him dwelleth all the fulness of the Godhead bodily. And ye are complete in him." I love the Authorized Version. I think there is no translation of the Bible remotely to be compared with it, but I have to say that it is a little unfortunate that the word used here is the word *complete*. The literal force of the original is easily retained and teaches a very valuable lesson: "In Him dwelleth all the fulness bodily. And ye are made full in Him." That is what Paul is saying. In ourselves we are poor, destitute, and empty, but we are made full in Him who is the very fulness of God manifest in the flesh. Paul took up the same theme in Ephesians 1:3. He says that we are blessed "with all spiritual blessings in heavenly places in Christ." Then follows an amazing list of blessings. There is a saying that familiarity breeds contempt, but I try never to develop that kind of familiarity with Ephesians 1. I memorize it, learn it, study it, pray over it,

49

and meditate upon it. I consciously seek to govern my thinking by what this passage teaches, and, thank God, it never loses its lustre. It never fails to rejoice my soul to think that I have been blessed with every spiritual blessing in heavenly places in Christ. I find it a wonderful stimulus to spiritual worship. When a man sees that he is poor in spirit but rich in Christ, he can be nothing but an admirer, a praiser, a worshipper, and a witness of Jesus Christ. I am worried about people who have little to say of Jesus Christ. When a preacher preaches nothing of Christ I have to wonder how much he knows of Christ. I have had people come to me over the years of my ministry and talk about their minister. I ask them if he is saved. "Well, I don't know. He seems to be a good man, but I don't know." There is something radically wrong with a man if you can sit and listen to him for five or ten years and you cannot be sure if he is saved. If a man has been brought to the foot of the cross he can never be anything but an exalter of Christ. Jesus Christ is all.

Consequently, the man who is poor in spirit will be *totally dependent on Christ and therefore will be much before His throne of grace in prayer.* The Lord Jesus said, "Without me ye can do nothing." The poor in spirit have that attitude when they first come to Christ for salvation, and they retain that same attitude of dependence on the Saviour in their Christian pilgrimage. If you are poor in spirit you will recognize that without Christ you can do nothing, and you will often be found at His feet. One of the loveliest pictures in the New Testament is of Mary of Bethany. I remember how it thrilled my heart the first time I saw this picture in the Bible. What do we know about Mary? She lived in Bethany. She was the sister of Lazarus and of Martha. She anointed the Lord Jesus. But what do we really know about her? We could speak with blessing of her faith and her tender-heartedness, but the greatest insight into the character of Mary is that every time she appears in the New Testament Scriptures she is at the feet of Jesus. When you are poor in spirit, that is where you will be. You will often approach the throne of grace. Feeling your personal emptiness and uselessness, you will long for the fulness that is in Jesus Christ, and you will therefore come boldly to the throne of grace to obtain mercy and to find grace to help in time of need.

These, then, are the marks of the poor in spirit.

The Mercy Shown to the Poor in Spirit

Notice the mercy shown to the poor in spirit— "Theirs is the kingdom of heaven." What a wonderful statement! What is the kingdom of heaven? I am not now going to give you a theological discourse on that subject about which so much contradictory material has been published. All I will say at this time is that the kingdom of heaven basically is that spiritual kingdom, whether in this world or the next, over which Jesus Christ is King. It is the mediatorial kingdom of Christ. What then is the kingdom of heaven? It is the kingdom of grace now and glory to follow, and it all stands on the merits of the Lord Jesus Christ.

That means that as soon as a man is brought in poverty of spirit to the Lord Jesus, *he at once becomes a subject of King Jesus.* Though the world derides the very idea, Christ is our King. If you have learned your Shorter Catechism—and if you have not there is no time like the present for starting!—you will know that it shows from Scripture that Christ our Redeemer occupies and exercises three functions, or offices. He is our Prophet, our Priest, and our King. And how does He execute the office of a king? Let me give you the catechism answer and its Scripture proofs: "Christ executeth the office of a king, in subduing us to Himself (Acts 15:14, 16), in ruling (Isa. 33:22) and defending us (Isa. 32:1, 2), and in restraining and conquering all His and our enemies (Psa. 110; I Cor. 15:25)." Mark well the working of Christ our King: 1) He subdues us to Himself; 2) He rules and defends us; 3) He restrains and conquers all His and our enemies.

Thus the kingship of Jesus Christ brings us into subjection to the will of God and keeps us safely under the power of His royal sceptre, despite the prevalence of the corruption of the old man and despite every device of the world and the devil to destroy the work of grace in us. It is good to know that the Lord is on the throne. When the devil is opposing you and the world hates you, how encouraging it is to know that the Lord is defending you and will with His almighty power restrain and conquer all who are His and your enemies.

What is this saying? It is saying that the believer is totally under the care of the Lord Jesus Christ. That is what it is to have Christ as your King.

Ultimately a king must be responsible for the safety and well-being of every one of his subjects. That is exactly the case with Christ. He has made Himself responsible for the well-being of every subject of His kingdom. That is why Paul could say, "My God shall supply all your need." When you know that the Lord cares for you, that the Lord has His hand upon you, that the Lord is going to restrain and defeat every power of earth and hell that can ever be ranged against you—when you know that God has made Himself responsible to keep you now and present you faultless in glory—then, my friend, you can rest at peace in Jesus Christ. You are brought into the kingdom of His grace and are the object of His constant protection, support, and sustenance. There is no power among devils or men that can frustrate the gracious purpose, or overcome the almighty power, of our King. What a confidence we have in Christ!

Christ's kingdom is different from any other in one very important respect: *as soon as you become a subject in it you become a king.* Thomas Watson rightly remarked, "All Christ's subjects are kings." Revelation 1:5, 6 records the song of the people of God here on earth. They are singing "unto him that loved us, and washed us from our sins in his own blood, and hath made us kings and priests unto God." Revelation 5:10 records the song of the saints in heaven. They are also singing unto the Lamb of God, who has "made us unto our God kings and priests: and we shall reign on the earth." Here then is the testimony of all the people of God, and it is exactly what the Lord Jesus promises when He pronounces the blessing, "Theirs is the kingdom of heaven." When God finds you poor in spirit, absolutely destitute, on the verge of a lost eternity in outer darkness, He lifts you up and makes you a veritable king. In Revelation 3:21 the Lord Jesus describes this kingly privilege in glorious terms: "To him that overcometh will I grant to sit with me in my throne, even as I also overcame, and am set down with my Father in his throne." That is what it is to be a king: reigning with Christ. Some of you can remember before you came to Christ how you were crushed with great sin and broken by overwhelming habits. There was nothing you could do to break the fetters that bound you. But now you rule the things that once ruled you. Why? Because you suddenly developed a new personality or a stronger will, or you learned a new set of rules to live by? No, sir! Because of the gracious power of Christ your king. This is the blessing—the mercy—shown to the poor in spirit.

This mercy *reaches its climax when we get to glory.* Peter gives us a beautiful description of the kingdom in II Peter 1:11, where he calls it "the everlasting kingdom of our Lord and Saviour Jesus Christ." Bless God, that is where His people belong, the sphere of their enjoyment for all eternity. When the Lord Jesus says, "Blessed are the poor in spirit," He speaks nothing more than the simple truth. "I found them," says He, "destitute and helpless. I saved them, I brought them under the power of grace, and I will bring them into the enjoyment of everlasting glory." That is the mercy He shows to the poor in spirit.

THE MESSAGE OF THE POOR IN SPIRIT

Now let us quickly consider the message of the poor in spirit. It is a message for both sinners and saints. Consider first the message to those who are not saved.

If you are unsaved, please notice very carefully that it is the poor *in spirit* who are blessed. No other kind of poor person is blessed. There is no particular blessing in poverty. Neither is there any particular shame in it. But there is a particular blessing for the poor in spirit.

There is a world—nay, an eternity—of difference between the poor in spirit and the spiritually poor. There are many who are spiritually poor, but they are very far from being blessed. They are like the rich man in Luke chapter 12. They gather what they can of this world's goods about them and give themselves over to the pursuit of earthly happiness based on mere possessions. However, God says, "Fool! With all your possessions you are not rich toward God." It does not matter what possessions you have, or what level of popularity you enjoy, or what success you attain in this life. It does not matter what reputation you may build for yourself among men, if you are not rich toward God—if you are not an heir of the kingdom, if you have not been washed in the blood of the Lamb, if you have not been brought to your knees at the foot of the cross—then you are not blessed. Those who are not rich toward God are called fools, for only a fool hastens toward eternal misery while boasting of the joy of worldly possessions that pass away more quickly than the morning dew. To such people Jesus said, "Thy soul shall be required of thee." If that should ever happen to you, which God forbid, you will feel for all eternity the difference between being poor in spirit and spiritually poor.

There is also a great difference between being poor in spirit and being poor-spirited. There are all too many poor-spirited people. They hear the gospel. They know the way of truth. They understand the call of God and feel in their soul something of the power of that call. They are moved. I have seen some of them moved to tears. I have seen them leave the church service reeling as if they were drunk under conviction of sin through the preaching of the gospel. But they do not come to Christ because they fear the blast of the world's opposition. As one old preacher put it, "They will dance to the devil's pipe if their superior commands it." Since the world calls out to them, they are not willing to take their stand with Christ. They are not willing to go the way of the gospel. So they dance to the devil's tune. Oh, they know the truth, but they are poor-spirited people, not needy souls who are poor in spirit. They are far from blessed.

There are thousands of poor, deluded souls across the world who have believed the Romish gloss upon this passage. They think that if they renounce their worldly goods and enter a cloister with a vow of voluntary poverty, they will be blessed on that account. My friend, salvation is not to be merited either with money or with the lack of it. It is by grace through faith. That is clear from our text. This word of Christ's is addressed not to works, but to faith.

The same is true throughout the Beatitudes. They are all addressed to faith. Human logic does not endorse one word of what Jesus says here. Human reasoning contemptuously rejects His evaluation. He says, "Blessed are the poor in spirit." That is anathema to human thinking, but it is refreshing news to faith. Faith rejoices in a message for sinners devoid of all merit, a message that says, "You have no standing except as a justly condemned sinner before God. But Christ has all the merit you need to be accepted of God, and His merit is imputed to those who receive Him by faith without works. Therefore confess your emptiness and call on Him to save you, and you will at once be brought into the number of those He pronounces blessed." Do not miss the blessing of free grace because of some foolish idea of making yourself worthy of it by any human effort. Grace is like the altar of which the Lord spoke to Moses: "If thou lift up thy tool upon it, thou hast polluted it" (Exod. 20:25). It is Christ a poor sinner needs, not a cloister. It is His merit, not your misery, that saves. The poor in spirit cast themselves totally upon Him in all His fulness. Do not try to substitute mere human self-denial, however beautiful that may be in other contexts, for the saving merit of Christ.

There is a kingdom to be had. Oh, that you would realize this! As you ponder eternal things and weigh the claims of the gospel, the devil brings before you the tantalizing attractions of the world—its promises, its pleasures, and its treasures. Remember, there is a kingdom at stake here, a kingdom of grace now and glory hereafter. At stake is a life that is worth living here and now. Beyond this life is an eternal escape from hell and an entrance into—and enjoyment of—glory for all eternity. There is a kingdom at stake. It may be had for all who will take Christ on His terms. Will you take Him that way? "Blessed are the poor in spirit: for theirs is the kingdom of heaven." I pray God that He will bring all who read these words to the end of themselves and their own resources. Will you come to the feet of Christ to receive His salvation by faith alone, on the sole merits of His blood and righteousness?

Once you receive Christ as your Saviour, you have His promise and assurance of blessing. He says, "Blessed are the poor in spirit." Your salvation depends, not on what you have done, or can do, or will do, but on the merits of Jesus Christ alone. When did you receive salvation? When by grace you fell on your face before God, poor and destitute, and He saved you because of what His Son had done at Calvary, not because of anything in you yourself. So your salvation depends on Christ, and nothing can rob you of a place in heaven. Jesus said, "Theirs is the kingdom of heaven." In Luke 12:32 the Lord Jesus says, "Fear not, little flock; for it is your Father's good pleasure to give you the kingdom." Ponder this very carefully. Fear not, for it is the Father's sovereign will—that is the meaning of His "good pleasure"—to give you the kingdom. Believers are like a little flock, poor, helpless, and apparently so easily overcome. But Jesus says, "Fear not. You will assuredly reach heaven."

What a blessing it is to have Christ! Though Satan may roar and temptations oppress, though the flesh may be weak and faith may falter, Jesus Christ never changes. We are not saved because of our hold on Christ, but because of Christ's hold on us. He will give us the kingdom. Therefore let us stay low at Jesus' feet, for that is where every blessing is received and enjoyed. As you stay low at Jesus' feet you will be enabled to walk worthy of the King whose Name you bear. Indeed, you will be empowered to walk as a king, exercising dominion in the might of the Spirit over the world, the flesh, and the devil.

CHAPTER FIVE

Blissful Mourners!

Blessed are they that mourn: for they shall be comforted.
Matthew 5:4

The Lord Jesus was undoubtedly the master of the unexpected. His messages were free from clichés and hackneyed phrases, and He made every single word count in His preaching of the gospel. Those who came to arrest Him confessed, "Never man spake like this man." Men hung upon His every word for the very good reason that every word came with surprising and amazing power.

This truth is beautifully illustrated for us in the Beatitudes. The Lord Jesus sits down upon the mountain to preach. The people gather around. Whereas Moses from the mount brought the word of the law with a curse and a condemnation, the Greater than Moses begins His ministry with a blessing on His lips. Does He say, "Blessed are the rich, the powerful, the religious"? Ah, no! Here you have the unexpected. "Blessed are the poor in spirit." And having surprised his audience with that first Beatitude, He goes even further in the next one and says, "Blessed are they that mourn." I think we can very easily miss the full force of that by maintaining the word *blessed*. It simply means "happy"—"Happy are they that mourn." Here indeed is a paradox: happy mourners. That paradox becomes all the more startling when you notice the strength of the word translated "mourn." It indicates passionate grief. There is an entirely different word that indicates grief which may be deep down in the heart but which may be hidden. We have all had experience of that kind of grief ourselves, or we have seen it in others. It is when someone has a grief deep down in his soul but puts on a brave face and wears an air of jollity, even though he is hurting deep inside. That is not what the Saviour is speaking about here.

57

The word here is of an altogether different meaning and significance. John Chrysostom, who was one of the greatest preachers of the ancient Greek church, said that the Greek word here speaks of those who grieve so that their grief is manifested externally. This is a grief that bursts forth with external manifestations, and yet the Lord Jesus says, "Happy are they that mourn." A paradox indeed.

Very clearly, this is not true of all kinds of passionate grief, or mourning. There are certain types of mourning that are far from being pronounced blessed of God.

Some men mourn because a curb has been placed upon their ungodly lusts. In II Samuel 13 you will read the disgraceful story of Amnon, the son of David, who made himself sick because of his ungodly lust after Tamar. He grieved so bitterly that he took to his bed, but his was not a mourning that produced any blessing. When a man's mourning is but the expression of his own sinful lust and his own ungodly heart, it is a devilish mourning. There is not the smallest seed of blessedness in it. There is a similar story in the case of Ahab, the man who sold himself to do evil more than all the other kings of Israel. Ahab again made himself sick by his grieving. He turned his face to the wall like a petulant child. He would neither eat not drink. He was in great heaviness of spirit. Why? Because he could not indulge his lust for added acquisitions. Naboth would not let him have his vineyard, part of his family's inheritance. So Ahab became deeply depressed. How many people today are doing the very same thing. They have themselves worried sick, they are in deep grief, simply because they cannot acquire what they have selfishly lusted after. My friend, that kind of grief produces no blessedness. It is rather a cancer in the soul. It will corrupt you more and more. It is a sin that needs to be grieved over and repented of.

Then there are some who mourn because of judgment on their sin. You remember the story of Cain in Genesis 4. He murdered his brother. He sought to introduce a new way to heaven. He despised the blood of the sacrifice. He brought down upon himself the just vengeance of God. In verse 13 we find him mourning. Does he lament that his hand spilled the blood of his innocent brother? Does he lament that he put away the blood of the sacrifice? Does he lament that he insulted God with the cursed religion of his own self-righteous work? No, sir! He looks God in the face, and he mourns that God judged his sin. He says, "My punishment is greater than I can bear." Many a soul weeps bitter tears because of the harvest of sin, while all the time longing for the sin itself. Instead of repudiating the sin, Cain embraced the sin, and all that he mourned about was the judgment of God. There are millions in the world just like Cain. They have no deeper sorrow than Cain. Perhaps even in this meeting there are some whose only real regret is the sword of judgment against their sin. There has never been one moment's revulsion against the sin itself. There is no blessedness in that kind of mourning. It rather holds a curse within it.

There are others who mourn because they have helped others to hell. They have grief and bitterness of soul because of their part in breaking lives and damning souls. I think of the rich man in Luke chapter 16 as he cries, "I have five brethren. We ate together; we drank together; we revelled together; we caroused together; we sinned together; we trod the road to hell together. Mine was the hand to help them downward. Mine was the advice that led them devilward." How deep must be the agony of a soul when the awful crime of dragging souls to perdition is brought home to it! Are there not countless multitudes of fathers, mothers, brothers, sisters, and friends who endure the same agony as the rich man of whom Jesus spoke? What an awful responsibility to have used the position of trust and power God gave you to lead immortal souls to ruin! My friends, I tell you, people who have helped souls to hell have good cause to grieve, but there is agony, not blessing, in such grief.

Then there are souls who mourn because they are in hell. I have mentioned the rich man in Luke 16. "I am tormented in this flame," said he. The Lord Jesus spoke of people who would mourn with weeping and wailing and gnashing of teeth. Nowadays even preachers who ought to know better downplay the awful reality of the torments of hell, but nothing can blunt the Saviour's warning that there is mourning in hell. But no blessedness results from the tormented grief of the eternally lost.

So Christ's words in our text are not a blanket description of all mourning. There are certain types of mourners who have no blessing in their tears. However, there is a mourning which, though deep and passionate in its grief, is yet blessed of God. I think I may call it "gospel mourning." That is what the Lord Jesus is speaking about— **gospel mourning and its blessed results.**

GOSPEL MOURNING BLESSES THE BEREAVED

Gospel mourning brings blessings to those who lament in the presence of death. The basic force of the word *mourn* in this passage, just as in English, is "to lament because of death." That is its most natural meaning. You may remember Solomon's very strange-sounding statement in Ecclesiastes 7:2: "It is better to go to the house of mourning, than to go to the house of feasting." Not a man in a million would agree with Solomon. In fact there are very few Christians who would agree with him here. But these are not just the words, as some say, of an embittered cynic. Solomon had enough to be cynical about, but these are not the words of an embittered cynic. These are the words of a man endued with divine wisdom, and he says that it is better to go to the house of mourning than to go to the house of feasting. By nature we would all rather go to the party where there is food and drink and laughter and conversation that will delight our hearts. Thus this word stands out like a beacon light. Choose rather the house of mourning. Why? The reason is very simple. It is this. The atmosphere in the house of feasting can very easily dull the senses to things that are eternally important. "The harp, and the viol, the tabret, the pipe, and wine, are in their feasts: but they regard not the work of the LORD, neither consider the operation of his hands" (Isa. 5:12). Conversely, when a man is face to face with death and with the loss of a loved one, he can learn some of the most valuable lessons of life. I think these lessons of the house of mourning need to be learned in our day. There is a tendency today to reduce Christianity to the inane grin, the plastic smile, the counterfeit happiness, the carnal euphoria. Have you noticed that the "in" phrase of so many professing Christians is "I'm excited"? A few years ago it was "born again." It seemed to be on everybody's lips. At least that was a Biblical expression, although it was very sadly perverted by people who all too often knew nothing about the Biblical reality of the new birth. Now the word is *excited*. "We have a new ministry—or a new method, or a new programme, or a new kind of church service—and I'm excited about it." It appears not to matter whether there is anything in the Bible to sanction it, whether God the Holy Ghost has pronounced His blessing or His curse on it. "I'm excited about it," and that means everything. I read recently of an alleged upsurge of evangelicalism in England, an evangelicalism that replaced the old *kerygmatic* —that is, the gospel preaching—function of worship with group involvement in song and dance. This is more exciting and attractive, especially to today's young people. Far from being a revival to boast about, this sounds very like mere carnal euphoria. In such days as these we can be easily misled into thinking that mourning has no part in Bible Christianity. It has. In the house of mourning we can learn some urgently needed lessons.

We learn the lesson of *the brevity of life*. I would to God that every healthy young man, woman, and child in this meeting would go to the house of mourning to look upon the stiff, cold corpse and see the reality of death and the brevity of life. I wish that people who are living without a thought of the end of life or the greatness of eternity would betake themselves to the house of mourning and learn the blessed lesson that life at best is very brief.

Life is not just one big party. Life is not what the ungodly and the sensual crowd want you to believe it is. There is a solemnity to life. Oh, there is joy for a Christian. The greatest happiness is in Christ. The first word in our text is *happy*; so I am not against God's people being happy. I simply want you to be sure that your happiness is grounded on a true foundation. There is a solemn side to life. *The solemnity of life is the reality of death,* for it is appointed unto each one of us once to die. The time will surely come when with a mighty sweep the scythe of death will cut you down.

You need to face that dread reality, because *beyond death there is judgment.* I tell you, when a man looks on the face of the corpse of his friend and his heart is broken at the thought of the parting, he can think more clearly then about judgment and eternity than when his ears are deafened with the raucous din of the world's entertainment in the house of feasting.

When you go to the house of mourning you are more likely to think of *the destiny of the soul*. I often think of Job's words: "Man dieth, and wasteth away: yea, man giveth up the ghost" —and then the greatest question you can ever ask of any man— "and where is he?" Where is he? He is somewhere. Death cannot annihilate the soul. It will live forever. But where? That is the question. According to the Word of God it will live forever in heaven or in hell. When you enter the presence of death you are forced to face the issue of your eternal destiny. It is a wise man who looks on the corpse of another and asks himself the searching question, "If it were my body lying in this casket, where would my soul be for eternity?" Do you see now why Solomon said, "It is better to go to the house of mourning"? There your mourning, by the grace of God, may be blessed to teach you the lessons you need to learn.

Think of a New Testament text, I Thessalonians 4:13-18: "But I would not have you to be ignorant, brethren, concerning them which are asleep, that ye sorrow not, even as others which have no hope. For if we believe that Jesus died and rose again, even so them also which sleep in Jesus will God bring with him. For this we say unto you by the word of the Lord, that we which are alive and remain unto the coming of the Lord shall not prevent [or precede] them which are asleep. For the Lord himself shall descend from heaven with a shout, with the voice of the archangel, and with the trump of God: and the dead in Christ shall rise first: then we which are alive and remain shall be caught up together with them in the clouds, to meet the Lord in the air: and so shall we ever be with the Lord. Wherefore comfort one another with these words." Here is mourning, Christians sorrowing, but, says Paul, there is blessing in their mourning. They do not sorrow as people who have no hope, for in the gospel God has brought life and immortality to light. Christ has died. Christ has risen. Christ is coming again, and those who sleep in Jesus God will bring with Him. So even in our deepest bereavement we have rest and comfort because of our hope of the return of Christ and of our reunion with all our departed loved ones in Him. Gospel mourning brings blessing to those who lament in the presence of death.

GOSPEL MOURNING BLESSES THE PENITENT

Gospel mourning brings blessing to all who lament over sin. That is the chief emphasis of the Lord Jesus here in Matthew 5:4. *Every man among us has cause to lament over his own sin.* Ezekiel 7:16 has a telling phrase: "All of them mourning, every one for his iniquity." Every one of us then has cause to lament his own sin.

There is the sin of ungodliness. That is the sin of nature. Jonathan Edwards describes it as a fire of iniquity, of wicked rebellion against

God—such a fire that if God did not moment by moment restrain it, would even now burst forth in all its hellish fury and consume the soul and bring it to the very depths of perdition without delay. Is it not true that every man amongst us has cause to mourn this innate ungodliness? Do you not find within you that law of sin, that nature of wickedness, that natural proclivity to evil, that bias to all that is iniquitous, that love of what is unrighteous and ungodly? There is that within every one of us that would reach up with Satan to seek to dethrone God, that would call God's Word a lie while embracing the devil's lie as the truth. There is an evil, vicious, diabolical, hellish wickedness residing in us all by nature. There burns in every breast the very fire that is kindled in outer darkness. There is not a man amongst us who has cause to be proud or to deck himself out in the robes of his own self-righteousness and parade himself before God with the attitude, "I am not as other men are." We are all just as vile by nature as the worst of men. Paul said that our carnal mind is enmity against God and cannot be made subject to His law (Rom. 8:7). Recognizing that, when you see the wickedness and the ungodliness that are everywhere apparent, you will understand that the vilest offender has a heart that is not one whit more depraved, or more wicked, or more godless than yours. How thankful we should be for restraining grace. Where would you have been had not God kept you back? If God had given you up to the natural lusts of your heart and of your mind—and this is applicable to the unsaved as well as the saved among us—where would you have been? Had God given you over to allow your lusts to lead you wherever they and the devil would take you, to what depths would you not have sunk? I tell you, my friend, you would already have burst out of this body into the depths of a lost eternity, down with the most depraved of men and with the devils themselves.

Every man amongst us tonight would do well to mourn because of sin. We live in a day when there is little preaching on sin, a day of easy believism and shallow preaching, a day when preachers want to make their ministry appear successful by obtaining "decisions" for almost any reason under the sun. If they fail to have people come forward to say, "I want to be saved," they will change the basis for their appeal so as to induce as many as possible to make some sort of public response. What a far cry from the old days of preaching! When Edwards preached on "Sinners in the hands of an angry God," men felt their sin and, smitten with deep conviction, wept their way to the cross. The old preachers so preached against sin that sinners were shaken to the core and trembled at the thought of their wickedness in the sight of a holy and righteous God. Such mourning was blessed, for under its influence they sought Christ. Oh, how men need to learn to mourn for sin, each man for the plague of his own ungodliness.

Not only must we mourn over an ungodly nature, but also over the consequent *unrighteousness, the actual wickedness,* it produces. There is a difference between ungodliness and unrighteousness. Ungodliness is the root; unrighteousness the fruit. Not only the root but the fruit needs to be lamented and repented of. "Fools make a mock at sin" (Prov. 14:9). Fools make light of sin. Fools gloss over sin. Fools hide sin. It is a wise man who takes to himself what the Bible says about his sin and laments over it. It is wise because Jesus says to those who with gospel mourning lament over their sin, "Blessed are they that mourn: for they shall be comforted."

Not only has every man amongst us cause to lament over his own sin, but surely we have cause—and this is especially true of Christians—to *lament over what sin is doing to others.* Can any Christian sit unmoved by the tragedy being enacted all around him? Can he look out upon the great multitudes of lost men and women without mourning what sin is doing? I fear that many professing Christians can. They can look at fathers and mothers, husbands and wives, brothers and sisters, even their own children, whom sin is destroying, with little or no compassion. They can condemn them, but do they ever weep for them?

How can we look out upon souls who are destroyed by sin and not mourn? Consider our land. Only God knows the depth of its filth and its folly with its drug addicts, its drunkards, its harlots, its abortionists and their victims, its broken hearts and broken homes. We all have our trite little answers, but so often they have little or nothing of the gospel in them. It is easy to point the finger of condemnation—and we must honestly identify the guilt of sin; there is no hope for a sinner if we pretend his sin is less than damning—but if all we do is point the finger, we are more like Pharisees than like Christ. We need a heart that feels deep sorrow for what sin is doing to its perishing victims. Until God's people start to mourn for the ungodly, I do not believe that the ungodly are going to mourn for themselves. Jeremiah said, "Oh that my head were waters, and mine eyes a fountain of tears, that I might weep day and night for the slain of the daughter of my people!" (Jer. 9:1). Look across your country with all its wealth, all it amusements, and all its entertainments, and see the slain, the souls that are being murdered by sin. Should we not mourn?

Should we not also mourn and lament *the sinful compromise and powerlessness of God's church in the midst of all this need?* If ever there were a day when God's people needed to walk in devotion to Christ and know the power of God the Holy Spirit, this is the day. Yet what do we find? Compromise. It is easy to criticize other people's compromise. I am a Biblical Fundamentalist, but I must confess that some Fundamentalists are too inclined to label everybody who does not cross their *t's* and dot their *i's* a compromiser. It is always easy to highlight somebody else's compromise. What about yours? What about mine? What about compromise with the world? There are Christians who have reached the stage where they can rationalize any sin. I have gone into Christian homes and have seen Christians watching things on television that a few years ago would have made a harlot blush. There can be no doubt about the sinfulness of their action, but they rationalize it. This is compromise; it is wickedness. I have cited only a very obvious example of Christians' compromise; there are endless others, for a worldly spirit is rampant in the church today. Nehemiah wept because the walls of Jerusalem were broken down and the gates thereof were burned with fire. There was nothing to stop the enemy from going in with his devastating fury against the cause that was dear to the heart of the man of God. And so he wept. If Nehemiah had reason to weep, what should be our response to the equally appalling condition of so many churches today? Do we not need to mourn? Thomas Watson said, "Sin must have its tears." May the Lord give us a broken and contrite heart over our evil compromise.

Gospel Mourning Points Us to Christ

If God has convicted you so that you are crying out to Him, "I am a sinner unclean and undone," or if God has broken your heart with the conviction that you are a backslider compromising with the world and with sin, let me tell you that He means to bless you by causing you to mourn. The blessing of gospel mourning is that it brings us to the end of ourselves and casts us totally on Christ and on His promise.

There are some who mourn with the mourning of despair. Judas did that, and he went out and hanged himself. He never got beyond his own wretchedness. There was no blessing there.

There are some who mourn with a fruitless grief. Esau did that. He had sold his birthright but later wanted to reach back through the years, pick up the broken pieces, and live as if it had never happened. He could not do it. His is one of the saddest pictures in the Bible. I have had the bitter task of meeting people just like Esau who have wrung their hands in grief, but all their tears could not erase their past. I am thinking of a young man whose life was marred forever. He sat in my study twisting his hands, weeping with convulsive grief, "Why did I do it? Oh, that it had never happened! How I wish I could go back." Fruitless grief. Esau was still profane; he still loved his sin, despite his tears. It is fruitless to wish you had not got into the mess you are in unless you turn to Christ, who alone can blot out the past and give you a new life.

There are some who mourn because of the price of sin, but they never turn from it. In II Corinthians chapter 7 there is a great contrast between gospel mourning and the sorrow of the world, which worketh death. Verse 10 reads, "Godly sorrow worketh repentance to salvation not to be repented of: but the sorrow of the world worketh death." There are many who feel sorry, who weep, but who will still have hell at the end of it. Tears do not wash away sin. "The sorrow of the world worketh death."

But gospel mourning leads to repentance. It brings a man to see his sin, to feel his sin, to face his sin, and to stop rationalizing away all his guilt. A man who is mourning in the sense that Jesus meant is a man who confesses, "Lord, I am guilty. I deserve to be damned to the very deepest hell. If You were to cast me into the deepest pit of outer darkness, I would have to confess even from there that You are righteous. I am at an end of myself. I am at an end of the indulgence of self. I am at an end of the righteousness of self. I am at an end of all hope in myself. But I throw myself completely on the Lord Jesus Christ and upon His promise." That is gospel mourning. There is the blessing of it. It brings a man right to the end of himself in order that it may cast him totally on the merits of the Lord Jesus Christ.

Do you mourn for sin? Are you cast down in sorrow because of your own wickedness, ungodliness, and unrighteousness? *Then let me tell you of Jehovah Tsidkenu, the Lord our righteousness,* Jesus Christ, who is made unto us wisdom, righteousness, sanctification, and redemption. In Christ there is cleansing from sin through the merit of His precious blood. In Christ there is a perfect righteousness, even the righteousness of His own perfect obedience, imputed to us. In Christ there is the peace of reconciliation with God. If you sorrow for sin, here is the gospel answer. Christ is all you need. He still receives sinners. He will not turn you away.

Are you a Christian sorrowing for lost souls? Then come to an end of yourself and plunge into the infinite resources of our Redeemer, for He is able to save to the uttermost. Do what the Lord Jesus commanded His disciples to do with the boy possessed with a dumb spirit: "Bring him unto me" (Mark 9:19). Let us bring the lost for whom we are burdened to Christ, pleading for their salvation and claiming His promise. He says, "Ask, and ye shall receive." Often we have not because we ask not. So let us ask, marshalling our arguments in prayer. Why should the devil claim our families to damn them in hell when God has said, "The promise is unto you, and to your children"? Why should we sit back and allow our loved ones to slide into the pit when His assurance is, "Believe on the Lord Jesus Christ, and thou shalt be saved, and thy house"? There are promises for us to claim if we are mourning over lost souls. Let us pray with confidence in the promises of God.

Do you sorrow for the state of the church? Or for the state of your own heart? Perhaps though you have come to Christ you feel you are now far from God, with no joy in the Lord, no up-to-date experience of the Lord, no daily going on with the Lord. The sad state of the church is reflected in the sad state of your own heart. If this is so, remember, "Blessed are they that mourn." Bring your backsliding to Christ, for the promise of His Word is, "If we confess our sins, he is faithful and just to forgive us our sins, and to cleanse us from all unrighteousness" (I John 1:9).

As far as the church is concerned, He has said, "I will build my church; and the gates of hell shall not prevail against it" (Matt. 16:18). We have good cause to mourn the spiritual condition of the church, but we have equal cause to take heart that He who shed His blood for her will ensure that His purpose of grace will not be frustrated. Let us take God at His Word and ceaselessly cry for a genuine revival. His promise holds good: "I will pour water upon him that is thirsty, and floods upon the dry ground: I will pour my spirit upon thy seed, and my blessing upon thine offspring" (Isa. 44: 3). The impotence of the church in the face of the deluge of satanic wickedness should not make us despair, but pray the more fervently for the fulness of the power of God to attend our ministry.

Do you sorrow in bereavement? It is a difficult thing to get over the ache of heart that follows the death of a loved one. If you have not yet experienced this pain, you soon will. The long shadow of death crosses every path. But Christ has said, "I am the resurrection, and the life: he that believeth in me, though he were dead, yet shall he live: and whosoever liveth and believeth in me shall never die. Believest thou this?" (John 11:25, 26). How do you answer the Lord's question? Do you believe this? Then stand upon it and be comforted by the sweet assurance of your Saviour, the conqueror of death and the destroyer of hell for all His people.

In the second Beatitude Christ has brought us into the house of mourning. Let us be sure to learn its lessons. By faith embrace Christ. Lean on Christ. Proclaim Christ. And though there will be much in this old world and much in your own heart to cause you grief, yet trusting and proclaiming Christ you will know blessing and comfort that the world can neither give nor take away.

Better still—there is always something better for the Christian; that is the great thing about God's salvation: however good it has been, however good it is, it is always better up ahead—better still, our prospect is one of happiness without tears. Consider two verses of Scripture. In John 16:20 Christ says, "Verily, verily, I say unto you, That ye shall weep and lament, but the world shall rejoice." Is that not what is happening today? But listen as our Lord continues: "And ye shall be sorrowful, but your sorrow shall be turned into joy." He puts it even more plainly in Revelation 21:4: "God shall wipe away all tears from their eyes." What are the causes of your tears? Death? There will be no more death in heaven. Sorrow? There will be no more sorrow. Crying? There will be no more crying.

Pain? There will be no more pain. "For the former things are passed away." Then will come to pass the full and eternal fruition of this glorious statement of the Saviour: "Blessed are they that mourn: for they shall be comforted." Then we will confess with rapture, "Blessed indeed was I to be a mourner in Zion, for I have been, I am, and I always will be eternally comforted."

> *O mourner in Zion, how blessed art thou,*
> *For Jesus is waiting to comfort thee now;*
> *Fear not to rely on the word of thy God;*
> *Step out on the promise—get under the blood.*

Good advice! May the Lord enable us all to step out on His promise and get under His blood.

CHAPTER SIX

Meek But Not Weak

Blessed are the meek: for they shall inherit the earth.
Matthew 5:5

T o the carnal mind meekness is weakness. It is mildness or gentleness in the extreme, even downright timidity. The common view is that a meek man is one who is sure to be trampled upon and ground into the dust. I suppose this is the understandable view of men in an age of great self-confidence, great self-assertion, and great self-justification. The words of the prophet Malachi are as appropriate today as in his time: "And now we call the proud happy" (Mal. 3:15). The Lord Jesus Christ certainly does not do so. On the contrary, He says, "Blessed are the meek"—not the proud or the self-sufficient, but the meek. By the word *meek* our Lord does not mean timid or spineless. In fact He means the very opposite, for according to Scripture the meek are strong in the Lord, enduring with great patience and firmness every difficulty which life can throw at them, keeping their eyes fixed steadfastly and unwaveringly on their Saviour. Basically the word *meekness* describes our attitude first to God and consequently to men, especially under pressure or suffering. In such times of adversity meekness describes a spiritual attitude to God and therefore a spiritual attitude to men. It is, if I could put it another way, a spiritual acceptance of God's dealings with us without bitterness or complaint. That is meekness.

Such an attitude is totally and absolutely foreign to human nature. We read in I Corinthians 2:14, "The natural man receiveth not the things of the Spirit." So when God deals with a man, his natural reaction is not acceptance, but rebellion. Romans 8:7 reveals that "the carnal mind is enmity against God: for it is not subject to the law of God, neither indeed

71

can be." The Lord Jesus summed it all up in John 14:17 when He spoke of the coming of the Holy Spirit, "whom the world cannot receive." Those are awful words. Properly understood, they describe total depravity more fully than even some of the more celebrated passages used in proof of the doctrine. The world cannot receive the Holy Spirit. What a summary of human wickedness! How it displays man's inbred hatred of God, his innate rebellion against God! When God the Holy Spirit comes among men—just as when God the Son came among men—their attitude is one of total and absolute rejection. They cannot receive Him.

Thus, when you discover meekness in a man, you are not dealing with a perfection in his nature or with some divine spark left within the natural man. You are dealing with something that is a gift of God, a direct working of the Holy Spirit in the life. In fact, Galatians 5:22, 23 states explicitly, "The fruit of the Spirit is . . . meekness." It is the gift or the grace of the Holy Spirit. It is wrought in us by the Holy Spirit to make us more like Christ, who said, "I am meek and lowly in heart" (Matt. 11:29).

When we read our text in the light of all this, we can see the reason for Christ's benediction. "Happy are those who accept the Lord's dealings without murmuring, bitterness, resentment, or complaining, for they shall inherit the earth"—a great text with a great truth, presenting what is surely a great need for every one of us. Therefore we are going to consider **meekness—how it works and what it obtains.**

MEEKNESS ACCEPTS THE LORD ON HIS OWN TERMS

Meekness accepts the Lord on His own terms. No man who is still living without Jesus Christ knows anything about meekness. The first thing that this gift of the Spirit does in a man is to open his heart to receive Christ—and to receive Christ on the terms upon which He is offered in the Scriptures. In other words, it leads a man to take God at His Word, to accept the plan of salvation without arguing or disputing and without seeking to trim it or cut parts out of it. Meekness simply accepts it without question, and in accepting the plan, it receives the Person presented in the plan. That is meekness.

There is a wonderful example of it in Acts chapter 10 in the story of Cornelius, the Roman centurion. He earnestly desired to be saved, and the

Lord instructed him to send for Peter, who would preach the gospel to him and give him words whereby he would be saved. Recounting this to Peter, Cornelius said, "Immediately therefore I sent to thee; and thou hast well done that thou art come. Now therefore are we all here present before God, to hear all things that are commanded thee of God" (Acts 10:33). This is the first step of meekness. "We are here before God to hear and to hearken to all God has to say." Cornelius was in effect bowing before the Lord, saying, "Lord, I want to be saved, and I do not care what it involves—what demands the gospel makes of me, what sin must be repudiated, what friends must be given up, what prosperity must be sacrificed. I do not care what it means to me in my job, whether it means that I lose my commission or suffer some other loss. I am before Thee a poor, trembling, guilty, hell-deserving sinner. I know that Thou hast revealed a way of salvation. I want God's salvation. I will take Christ on God's terms." There was no argument, no attempt to trim the gospel of salvation to a set of humanly acceptable standards.

I am concerned about people who say, "I want to be saved, but do I really have to give up this or that?"—as if they wished to have Christ on their terms, not God's. I have great fear for such people. I have even greater fear for the preachers who assure them, "No, no, don't worry about turning away from sin. Just come and believe on Jesus. Make Him your Saviour, and you can think later about making Him your Lord." To use the language of Christ, this approach will succeed only in making them "twofold more the children of hell." When a man is in earnest about getting right with God, when he is burdened about his sin, when he has seen the holiness of God, when he has recognized the reality of hell, when he has begun to value the precious shed blood of Christ, he falls low at the feet of Jesus and cries, "Lord, I must have salvation on Your terms. I take Jesus Christ as He is freely offered unto me in the gospel."

There is true repentance involved here, for, as I said a moment ago, this meekness is foreign to human nature. Rebellion is removed. Pride, self-confidence, and self-righteousness are all put away. The man to whom the Holy Spirit imparts meekness is willing to turn from sin and to receive Jesus Christ. This is the first step of meekness—it accepts the Lord on His own terms. Have you ever been brought to that place? Have you yet come to the end of yourself, or arrived at the place where you loathed yourself,

73

your sin, and the world? Have you ever seen yourself as a poor, wretched, guilty criminal in the sight of your God and felt yourself to be fit fuel for the fires of hell? Do you know anything of the conviction of the Spirit that wrings from the soul the confession, "Lord, You would be just if You were to damn me deeper down than Sodom and Gomorrah, or Tyre and Sidon"? Have you ever come to the place of recognizing your total ungodliness and, looking away to Christ as God's provision for salvation, have you ever cried, "Lord, I will take Jesus Christ on the terms upon which God offers Him to me"? This is the only way to be saved. Any decision made on any other basis is spurious, satanic, and counterfeit. This is the true action of faith and repentance. This is the first evidence of the grace of meekness. You would be foolish to comfort yourself that you are on your way to heaven if all you can say is, "I made a decision, but I have accepted Christ on my terms, not His. There is part of my heart deliberately locked to Him. There are certain sins I will not have Him save me from." Ah, you cannot have Christ on those terms. He is the Lord, and He must be your Lord if you are ever to be saved. Thomas cried, "My Lord and my God!" The meek man's heart echoes that cry, for the first mark of meekness is that it accepts Christ on God's terms.

MEEKNESS OPENS THE HEART TO GOD'S WORD

Meekness opens the heart to what the Lord has to say. "Wherefore lay apart all filthiness and superfluity [that is, the abundance or overflowing] of naughtiness [or malice], and receive with meekness the ingrafted [or implanted] word, which is able to save your souls" (James 1:21). When a man comes to Christ, his heart is open to the Word of God. No man has received Christ who rejects the Bible. This is God's Word, and it is this Word He implants in those He saves. You cannot receive the incarnate Word while rejecting or repudiating the inscripturated Word. You cannot divorce them. When you come to Jesus Christ and accept Him on God's terms, your heart gladly embraces the Bible. Do not for a moment believe the devil's lie that it is scholarship or scientific research that makes men liberals and modernists. It is not. The greatest scholars who have ever lived have been devoted students of Scripture. Robert Dick Wilson, one of the greatest Semitic scholars America has ever produced, said that no man knew enough to be able to criticize one word of the Old Testament.

It is not scholarship that makes men unbelievers; it is sin, specifically the dark sin of pride. That arrogance that swelled first within the breast of Lucifer and now swells in the breast of every man in whom the devil holds sway is the real reason men reject the Bible. But when that man is brought to know Jesus Christ as his Saviour, not only does he accept Christ, but with meekness he receives the ingrafted Word of God. This Book in all its truth is implanted in his heart. The second thing, then, that meekness does is open the heart to what God has to say.

This is the attitude Eli taught to young Samuel: "Speak, LORD; for thy servant heareth." Visiting the home of a colleague at the time of family prayers, I was struck by a prayer of his children: "Lord, give me Samuel's ears." A good prayer. "Speak, LORD; for thy servant heareth." It indicates a heart that is open to the Word of God, a life that is regulated by the Word of God. This is true meekness. No man knows meekness who is not living by the Word of God. Moses is a great example here. Moses had difficulty in accepting the call of God, not through pride, but through fear. He felt he had failed once when he had tried to release the children of Israel from Egyptian bondage, and he was afraid to try again. The Lord overcame that natural fear and turned his timidity into meekness. That meekness was evidenced by his open-hearted obedience to the Lord's Word. When the Lord told him to do something, he did it. When the Lord commanded him to say something, he said it. Why? His heart was open to the Word of God, and his life was regulated by it.

Such meekness will answer many of the problems of everyday life. Christians live in a very complex world. How should we live? What should we do? The answer must always be, "Do what the Bible says." If you do not know what the Bible says on any given issue, take the time to find out, and then do it. No matter what it costs, even if it runs contrary to your most cherished notions, follow God's Word. That is how meekness works: it opens the heart to hear what God says.

MEEKNESS SUBMISSIVELY BOWS TO THE WILL OF GOD

Meekness embraces the will of God with a complete and yielding submission. Take Eli as an example. Through Samuel Eli received a message from the Lord, a message which must have brought great sorrow to his heart. His sons were about to perish for their sins. Eli may be blamed for many things, particularly his lack of parental discipline, but at least when the judgment of God was announced to him he showed true meekness. He said simply, "It is the LORD: let him do what seemeth him good" (I Sam. 3:18).

Contrast Jonah. Called to go to Nineveh as the prophet of the Lord, he refused and ran away. He took the longest route to Nineveh that anyone could take. He went via the belly of the whale. He would have been far better to have obeyed God in the first place. But Jonah was not meek at this time. His nationalistic pride was offended that God would send a prophet to Nineveh. To his way of thinking, the Assyrians should have been cursed of God without delay. He would have been happy to see God judge them. They did not need a warning or a prophet. Did they not pose a deadly threat to the promised land and the covenant people? Then let God curse them. God commanded Jonah, "Go and announce judgment." Jonah baulked at going because he feared the announcement of judgment might produce repentance and that the Lord would be merciful and grant pardon. Finally, with a very poor grace, he went. He did not preach one word of repentance, only judgment. There was not one word of comfort, only the stark message, "Yet forty days, and Nineveh shall be overthrown." At that point a wonderful thing happened. "So the people of Nineveh believed God, and proclaimed a fast, and put on sackcloth." Their king sent forth a proclamation: "Let man and beast be covered with sackcloth, and cry mightily unto God: yea, let them turn every one from his evil way, and from the violence that is in their hands. Who can tell if God will turn and repent, and turn away from his fierce anger, that we perish not?" (Jonah 3:5, 8-9). Here is a very humbling thing. These people turned in repentance to the Lord without any encouragement from the preacher. Souls are not saved by great sermons or by the preacher's engaging style. People are saved when God the Holy Spirit does His sovereign work. That is what happened in Nineveh. The Spirit wrought repentance. God gave them mercy, and Jonah was bitterly angry. He showed this a little later when the Lord destroyed a gourd under which the prophet was sheltering from the sun. Resentfully he cried out to God, "I do well to be angry, even unto death." People can become very bitter even against the Lord and speak very ill-advisedly, and often for the very same reasons as Jonah. They are angry at the seeming lenience of the Lord toward the ungodly and at the discomfort or pain they have to bear when He removes something in which they have found pleasure or comfort. It is just at this point that a meek spirit will save us from much trouble.

We have highlighted two extremes. Jonah arrogated to himself the position of knowing better than God. Eli bowed to the Lord's judgment and said, "Let the Lord do what is good in His sight." Every Christian needs to have the grace to accept the will of God as Eli did. Better still, he must seek to have the same submissiveness as the Lord Jesus Himself when He said, "Not my will, but thine, be done" (Luke 22:42). When He taught His people to pray, He gave them this petition: "Thy will be done in earth, as it is in heaven." To many Christians this prayer comes very easily. They think of it simply as a prayer about the end of the age, when the Lord returns. Very gladly they plead, "Lord, come and let Your will be done in earth." But let us not fool ourselves. Do you think for one minute that the Lord takes you seriously when you say, "Thy will be done in earth," if you are not willing to say, "Thy will be done in me as it is in heaven"? Christians should be marked by a sincere and submissive desire to do the will of God even as it is done in heaven. How is the will of God done in heaven? It is done perfectly, instantaneously, and joyfully. We are all too well aware that while we are in this body of humiliation we cannot do the will of God perfectly. But nothing would please us better than if we could. "Lord, let Your will be done in me as it is in heaven." That is true meekness.

As soon as Saul of Tarsus was saved he cried, "Lord, what wilt thou have me to do?" (Acts 9:6). If you have no heart to do the will of God or to please Christ, I doubt if you know Him at all. If you can be happy living a life displeasing to the Lord but pleasing to the devil, you need a new heart. The temporary failure of men like Jonah, inexcusable as it may be, pales into insignificance in comparison to what I can only term the official theology of wilful disobedience that is being promoted today. It is common for preachers to tell sinners to accept Christ as Saviour while deliberately rejecting Him as their Lord. This is what is meant by "easy believism," and it leaves a man with a decision that will take him to perdition. When a man receives Christ he does so meekly. That simply means that he has a heart for the will of God. When he fails and falters and stumbles, it grieves his soul, for his heart's desire is to do the will of God. "What wilt thou have me to do?" No excuses. No further questioning. No complaints. "I will run the way of thy commandments" (Psa. 119:32).

> *Where He may lead me I will go,*
> *For I have learned to trust Him so;*
> *And I remember 'twas for me*
> *That He was slain on Calvary.*
>
> *Oh, I delight in His command,*
> *Love to be led by His dear hand;*
> *His divine will is sweet to me,*
> *For I remember Calvary.*

MEEKNESS RESTS IN THE SOVEREIGNTY OF GOD

Meekness looks beyond men and circumstances and sees the sovereignty of God controlling every aspect of life. *It rests in the Lord and thereby avoids bitterness and frustration.* A meek man is a man who knows God is on the throne and in control of all things. Nothing can come into my life except the Lord commands it or permits it, and He controls it. Not a thing. No devil or man can do anything to me except the Lord allows it, and He controls it for my good and His own glory. That is a very practical statement of the sovereignty of God. Many people become very agitated when you talk about the sovereignty of God. To me it is the bedrock of faith. If God is not the absolute, sovereign ruler and disposer of all things, I have no hope of salvation. But He is! He is in control of the angels of heaven and all their actions. He is in control of all the demons of hell and all their actions. He is in control of all the men and all the armies of men on earth and all their actions. While men are responsible for their own sin, the Lord God Almighty is in total control. He makes even the wrath of men to praise Him (Psa. 76:10). I cannot explain how He does it. I feel no need to try. God defies explanation. If you have a little god whom you can neatly package and explain and put away in a little corner of your theological system, you are not a Christian, for you have denied the God of the Bible. God defies explanation. He is in control.

His dealings are always right and wise. He is rich in mercy. He loves us with an everlasting love. He has a Father's concern for His people. His eyes are upon us, and His ears are open to our cry. He therefore makes all things work together for our good. Knowing this, a meek man facing trying circumstances will look to the Lord and say, "Even so, Father: for so it seemed good in thy sight" (Matt. 11:26).

Let us now be very practical. One of the severest trials you are called upon to endure is when your fellow men are the direct cause of your sufferings, especially when they are malicious and unjust to you. It is hard to bear. The natural reaction is to be bitter and vengeful. One great preacher spoke of a Christian who said, "When people have hurt me so badly, I cannot give place to them." His reply was, "You had better, otherwise you will give place to the devil." It is hard to bear the slights and injuries men heap on us. But meekness looks beyond man, who is after all what the prophet called "the rod of God" in the situation, and sees the Lord. "This also cometh forth from the LORD of hosts, which is wonderful in counsel, and excellent in working" (Isa. 28:29). This is how meekness reasons. I am not saying that a meek man cannot take legitimate steps to redress the wrongs men do to him. That would be unscriptural and wrong. I am simply saying that he will seek to discern the hand of the Lord in it all and will submit every action and reaction of his to the revealed will and Word of God. The Lord's glory will mean more to him than mere personal vindication.

Each of us will have a situation in his own life to which he may apply all this. Some person or persons have done us injury in business, in the home, or even in the church. They have hurt us. We feel it. There is a natural bitterness, a natural desire for revenge, or at least for vindication. Many lasting wounds are inflicted in church and family situations because of implacable insistence on personal vindication, or because of an unwillingness to forgive or overlook real or imagined hurts. "Only by pride cometh contention: but with the well advised is wisdom" (Prov. 13:10). "The well advised" is the meek man. He stops before reacting in kind to his adversaries and reasons, "I do not excuse the sins of men, but I cannot suffer apart from God. This also cometh forth from the Lord of hosts, and He is excellent is His working. What would He have me to do or say in this situation?"

Thus *meekness turns us from hasty anger.* Ecclesiastes 7:9 speaks to this point: "Be not hasty in thy spirit to be angry: for anger resteth in the bosom of fools." Do we not need this rebuke? Do we not habitually rush to make a bitter and angry response when harmony in the home, the church, or the business—and especially the cause of Christ in these places—would be better served by a meek spirit that takes time to seek the Lord's will and way of addressing the problem? Have we not seen enough evidence of Christians who have had the momentary carnal satisfaction of an irate riposte only to regret that their folly injured their testimony and cost them the opportunity to be of service for Christ? "Be not hasty in thy spirit to be angry."

Meekness will also keep us from bitter vengefulness. In Romans 12:19 Paul says, "Dearly beloved, avenge not yourselves, but rather give place unto wrath: for it is written, Vengeance is mine; I will repay, saith the Lord." The world has a saying that should have no place in the heart of a Christian. It is, "I don't get mad; I just get even." I have known people to waste their lives and destroy any Christian testimony they had because they could not leave it to the Lord to vindicate them. Perhaps you are committing this very sin. You are harbouring spite in your heart against someone who has injured you and who has not yet paid sufficiently for it. This is like a cancer in your soul. It is doing unspeakable harm to you. It is robbing you of any spiritual joy or usefulness. You need to ask the Lord for the grace of meekness to resign it all to Him. He knows it all. He will vindicate the right and judge the wrong. Sink your futile wrath in the great ocean of the sovereign, wise, and good will of God.

Again, *meekness will save us from evil speaking.* Paul's admonition in Ephesians 4:31 is to put away evil speaking. There is far too much of this among professing Christians. Even the supposedly spiritual will use spiteful comments and innuendo to put down someone with whom they feel the need to get even. The answer to this evil is a meek spirit. The alternative is to be complaining, critical, and bitter, and there is nothing more unlike Christ, more obstructive to the testimony of the gospel, than this.

From all this you must see that *a meek man is strong in the face of provocation*. He is able to do two things. First, he will firmly hold to the truth of God—and to the God of truth. Meekness is not a spineless cowardice that runs and hides because it cannot stand up to opposition. Nothing could be further from the truth. The Lord Jesus was meek, and the zeal of God's house ate Him up, leading Him to confront the money-grasping hypocrites who had turned the house of God into a den of thieves. A meek man will stand for the truth of God, and He will stand for the God of truth. But—and this is the second thing a meek man is able to do—when he is provoked or suffers for his stand, he fixes his eyes on the Lord and does not allow the provocation or the pain to become a snare to make him sin. Of course, this is the devil's aim in all the opposition he engenders against God's people, to ensnare them into sin, to break their fellowship with their Lord. Meekness enables you to overcome this stratagem of hell, to look beyond your circumstances and rest secure in the sovereignty of God. He is in control. He will do right by you. There is no need for anger, bitterness, evil speaking, or anxiety. Keep these things before you and you will not be betrayed into sin by a carnal reaction to difficult circumstances.

MEEKNESS TREATS OTHERS AS GOD TREATS US

Meekness makes us treat others according to God's gracious dealings with our own souls. Follow Paul's reasoning in Titus chapter 3 very closely: "Put them in mind . . . to speak evil of no man, to be no brawlers, but gentle, shewing all meekness unto all men. For we ourselves also were sometimes foolish, disobedient, deceived, serving divers lusts and plea-sures, living in malice and envy, hateful, and hating one another. But after that the kindness and love of God our Saviour toward man appeared, not by works of righteousness which we have done, but according to his mercy he saved us, by the washing of regeneration, and renewing of the Holy Ghost; . . . that being justified by his grace, we should be made heirs according to the hope of eternal life" (vv. 1-7). Do you grasp the force of his argument? Treat men with meekness, because you were as guilty a sinner as any and are saved only by the grace of God. You have nothing at all of which to be proud. Yet Christians very easily fall into pride and set up double standards. They can look out on ungodly men and simply condemn them. No doubt their sin is to be condemned, but we should remember that we were not one bit better. Do not rise up on your high pedestal of self-esteem or look down the long nose of pride on the poor sinner. He needs the Christ who saved you. A humble remembrance of the grace of God toward us will impart meekness and lead us to confess, "I am what I am by the grace of God. The grace that saved me can save any man. Therefore my dealings with all men will be in the light of God's grace, God's love, and God's will. I will ever seek to be and to do whatever I can to help bring men to Jesus Christ." Paul instructed Timothy as to the duty of the Lord's servants: "In meekness instructing those that oppose themselves; if God peradventure will give them repentance to the acknowledging of the truth; and that they may recover themselves out of the snare of the devil, who are taken captive by him at his will" (II Tim. 2:25-26). Instruct them in meekness, if peradventure God will give them repentance. Why did you repent? I know that there is a theology running around today—I am tempted to say, crawling or creeping around; that may give a better clue to its genealogy!— which says that we all have the gospel preached to us. The only difference between you and the impenitent sinner is that you by the mere unfettered choice of your own will exercised repentance and he did not. It is just not true! He is to blame for not coming, but God has the glory for your coming. Let us not stand above a world of sinners, looking down upon them in pride and saying, "I heard the same gospel and I came." God gave you repentance. That is what this Bible says. And the God who gave you repentance can give repentance to the worst sinner in the world.

What are we to do? Are we, as so many Christians do today, to withdraw ourselves so that we do not soil our lily-white hands with contact with the sinners of this world? No, sir! We are to instruct them in meekness, if peradventure God will give them repentance. Meekness will enable us to treat men as God treats us. When that happens we will see the solution to a host of pressing problems. Take the example of the problems parents have rearing their children. Some parents fail to discipline their children at all; others go to the other extreme and batter them into senseless submission. How can you resolve such situations? Try treating them as God has treated you, and you will have the right balance between loving support and loving severity.

You can and should apply the same standard to every other problem area. Of course, sometimes it will appear that you are leaving yourself wide open to getting hurt again. Yes, you are. But there is a God in heaven, and He is in control—and He has said that the meek shall inherit the earth. God has promised His blessing on the meek: "Blessed are the meek." So many problems of bitterness and wrangling could be settled if we would only treat men as the Lord treats us. This is especially true in the church. Ephesians 4:32 puts it with powerful clarity: "Forgiving one another, even as God for Christ's sake hath forgiven you." This is how meekness works.

MEEKNESS IS A BLESSING IN ITSELF

The meek are greatly blessed. One of the chief blessings of meekness is meekness itself. Isaiah says, "The wicked are like the troubled sea, when it cannot rest, whose waters cast up mire and dirt. There is no peace, saith my God, to the wicked" (Isa. 57: 20-21). That is the picture of our state by nature. But when the Holy Spirit of God comes and imparts true meekness to us, we have peace—the peace of knowing the control of God, of knowing that He is working all things for our good, of knowing that He can and will look after every circumstance that hurts or challenges our lives. Psalm 37 discusses this peace in the midst of the hurts caused by evil men and difficult circumstances: "Fret not thyself because of evildoers, neither be thou envious against the workers of iniquity. . . . Trust in the LORD, and do good. . . . Delight thyself also in the LORD. . . . Commit thy way unto the LORD. . . . Rest in the LORD, and wait patiently for him: fret not thyself because of him who prospereth in his way, because of the man who bringeth wicked devices to pass. Cease from anger, and forsake wrath: fret not thyself in any wise to do evil. For evildoers shall be cut off: but those that wait upon the LORD, they shall inherit the earth. . . . The meek shall inherit the earth; and shall delight themselves in the abundance of peace" (vv. 1-11). What a blessing meekness is. By it you can live in peace in a restless world. It is a great source of peace to be able to say,

"Lord, I am where You placed me. I am Your blood-bought child, indwelt by Your Spirit and sealed unto the day of redemption. Lord, You have promised to look after me and all concerning me. I am facing hardship, misrepresentation, persecution, or some other affliction. You have told me not to fret or become bitter, to leave it all in Your hands. This I do by faith in Christ. I trust Your assurance that I shall yet delight myself in the abundance of peace and that You shall bring forth my righteousness as the light, and my judgment as the noonday. I cast my care upon You in the knowledge that You care for me."

Insoluble problems can be solved when they are handed over to the Lord. Remember, there is not a heart He cannot change, not a persecuting Saul He cannot make into a beloved Paul. There is not a mountain He cannot remove, not a devil He cannot defeat. Meekness rests on this assurance and enjoys great peace.

MEEKNESS LEADS TO THE ENJOYMENT OF EVERY OTHER BLESSING IN CHRIST

Finally, meekness leads to the enjoyment of every other blessing God has to give. Jesus says, "The meek . . . shall inherit the earth."

There is a prophetic statement here. The politicians of the world, the military leaders of the world, and the cults all have their plans for the world. They all have their ideas as to who will have a place in their brave new world. Hitler thought it would belong to his Aryan super race. The Russellites—the self-styled "Jehovah's Witnesses" (a worse misnomer would be difficult to imagine)—allocate it to the worthy and obedient who fail to make it into the number of the 144,000 who become Christ's heavenly bride. But Jesus says that the meek shall inherit the earth. This old earth—this is a large theological subject which I merely mention in passing—was included in the redemptive work of Jesus Christ. At the moment it groans as it awaits the adoption, the redemption of the body. But it does not belong to the communists or to the rest of the godless crowd who will ultimately perish from the earth. Our Saviour is coming in glory, and He will reign. We read in Daniel 7:21, 22 that the saints shall possess the kingdom. Bless God, the meek shall inherit the earth. According to Revelation 5:9, 10, the saints in heaven are singing, "Thou art worthy . . . for thou wast slain, and hast redeemed us to God by thy blood . . . and hast made us unto our God kings and priests: and we shall reign on the earth." I believe that to be a great prophetic statement. Only the meek will be there. The man whose heart has not been emptied at the cross to receive Christ on His own terms, whose heart has not been opened up to receive and be regulated by the Word of God, will not be there. There is no place with Christ in His kingdom for any but the meek. Thus meekness is not a perfection in saving grace, but is of the very essence of grace in the soul.

There is also a spiritual meaning to the statement, "The meek . . . shall inherit the earth." The word *earth* may be translated "land," and that would indicate the promised land. There is a picture here. The Old Testament spoke of the land of Canaan as the land of blessing. It is an Old Testament term that describes the New Testament blessings of the covenant of grace. What are those blessings? We are heirs of God. We are joint-heirs with Jesus Christ. We are blessed with all spiritual blessings in heavenly places. We have everything that pertains to life and godliness. This is a land of fatness, of fulness, and of plenty, a land that flows with milk and honey. It is the land in which the Lord smiles upon His people and they live in fellowship with Him in the power of His Holy Spirit. There is a higher plane of spiritual living than most Christians have ever dreamed. There are heights of love and depths of experience that, when compared with our present experience, are like Canaan in comparison to the wilderness. May God bring us into the enjoyment of Canaan fulness! It belongs to the meek. When we are found low at the feet of Jesus we have His promise that we shall enter in and inherit this land.

This is the working and the worth of meekness. As I said at the beginning, this is a gift and a grace of God. *If you are not saved,* but are now willing to take Christ on His terms, this is the grace of the Holy Spirit to you. Come with confidence and trust Him, and you will be saved. *If you have already come to Christ* and have received Him, cry for an increase of the grace of meekness. Your whole peace of mind and your prosperity in Christ depend on your being meek.

85

That raises the all-important question: If meekness is all that necessary, how can I be meek? Remember, it is a grace. Micah wrote, "Who is a God like unto thee, that pardoneth iniquity, and passeth by the transgression of the remnant of his heritage? . . . He will have compassion upon us; he will subdue our iniquities" (Mic. 7:18, 19). The Lord who saves also subdues the iniquities of His people. By grace we can be meek despite our natural bent in the opposite direction. Meekness is a part of the fruit of the Spirit (Gal. 5:23). How can you bring forth the fruit of the Spirit? By the Spirit. And the Spirit always works by revealing Christ to us. Every spiritual blessing comes back to Christ. He says, "Abide in me" (John 15:4). If you abide in Christ, you will bring forth fruit. If you abide in Christ, you will be meek. And if you are not meek, you are not abiding in Christ.

Do you ask, "How can I be meek?" The answer is clear. Look to Christ. Live on Christ. Lean on His sovereign power and love. He will produce the abundant harvest of this fruit in your life. He will give you grace calmly to trust Him. When the pressure of life mounts and you would naturally want to explode, you will be able to rest with calm assurance and say, "I have peace." Remember the promise of Psalm 37:11: "The meek shall . . . delight themselves in the abundance of peace." May God grant us a rich supply of the grace of meekness and a rich enjoyment of all the fruit it produces.

CHAPTER SEVEN

God's Banquet for Hungry Souls

*Blessed are they which do hunger and thirst after righteousness:
for they shall be filled.*
Matthew 5:6

I t is always a great blessing for a soul to feel its need. That is the first step in having the need met. God has a full provision for the needs of the human soul, and the only condition He places upon receiving it is to have an appetite for it. The blessing of God is given to any and all who have a stomach for it. It is one of the greatest evidences of the freeness of the gospel that the only condition the Lord Jesus sets on receiving eternal life and all the blessings that go with it is not penance or payment, but simply an appetite, a desire, for the blessing. No man will be lost who honestly desires to be saved. No soul will be left empty who earnestly yearns to be filled. The trouble with men is that they do not take the gospel seriously. The Lord Jesus says, "Blessed are they which do hunger and thirst after righteousness." Hungering and thirsting are expressive of the most vehement desire of which the human heart is capable. Sadly, however, carnal men are filled with sin and its pleasures. They have no taste for the things of God. As Paul put it to Timothy, they are "lovers of pleasures more than lovers of God." Thus if any man goes away from the Lord Jesus Christ unblessed, it is simply because he has no appetite, no pre-eminent desire for God's Son and God's salvation. If any man desires to be blessed, he may confidently rely on this promise of the Saviour: "Blessed are they which do hunger and thirst after righteousness: for they shall be filled." This is **God's banquet for hungry souls.** The text is one that can be applied to both saints and sinners, because the word *righteousness* is used in the Word of God in a very full and multi-faceted sense. Because of this extensive meaning we can take this little text of Scripture and see in it the fulness of the banquet of divine grace.

SINNERS HUNGER FOR THE IMPUTATION OF RIGHTEOUSNESS

Every convicted sinner feels his need of righteousness. When a man is brought face to face with God, he is convicted of sin. He is overwhelmed by a sense of guilt. He feels that he is a just object of the wrath of God. There is no more self-justification. There is no more vain excusing of sin, but rather a humble confession: "Lord, I am a vile and guilty sinner. I deserve the wrath of God. I feel myself as foul and full of sin as a man can be. If hell were to open up and swallow me at this very moment, it would be not one whit more than I deserve." Every convicted sinner is brought to face his sin and therefore to feel his need of righteousness. The Lord Jesus said, "When he [the Holy Spirit] is come, he will reprove [convince or convict] the world of sin, and of righteousness, and of judgment" (John 16:8). When God starts dealing with a man, that man feels, "I need righteousness, a perfect righteousness upon which to stand and with which to be clothed in the sight of God. I need a righteousness that will quiet the thunders of the law of God against me. *I need a righteousness that will satisfy that law from Mount Sinai* with its flaming wrath that would blaze upon my soul and bring me down to hell. That law condemns me. I need a righteousness that will meet the law, satisfy the law, and silence the law, so that for evermore Mount Sinai will not flash with lightning and sound with thunders to my destruction, but will rather be a witness that I am righteous and acceptable and fit for heaven." Nothing less than a righteousness that satisfies the law will do for us when we are convicted of our sin by the Holy Spirit.

We also need a righteousness that will still the turmoil of conscience. Every sinner knows what it is to have a conscience that accuses. The law that is written on the heart speaks even when you try to shut your ears to the Bible and turn away from the preaching of the gospel. Even when you try to silence the witness of God's Word and seek to immerse yourself in worldliness and selfishness, there is yet in your breast a witness which cries that you are guilty. Every man who feels this turmoil of soul is constrained to confess, "I need a righteousness, not only to quiet the thunders of Mount Sinai, but to still my own accusing conscience."

We also need a righteousness that will answer the accusations of the devil. He constantly seeks to resurrect our past. We have tried to forget it but cannot. We have tried to bury it as Abraham buried his dead, out of our sight. But, oh, we cannot do it, for Satan brings it up before us and torments us with its inexcusable nature and damning character. We need a righteousness that can shut the mouths of devils.

And we need a righteousness that then can enable and empower us to live a life of purity and of victory over sin in this world of corruption and lust. Salvation is not an easy matter. Now, do not misunderstand me. The way into salvation is simple, clear, and plain. You need be in no doubt as to how to be saved. Acts 16:31 is too plain to be misunderstood: "Believe on the Lord Jesus Christ, and thou shalt be saved." But salvation was not easily provided. I would reverently say that it plumbed the depths and scaled the heights of the entire wisdom and power of God. Only divine wisdom and power could produce a salvation that could save sinners, justify the ungodly, satisfy God and His law, silence the devil and his accusation, still the conscience, and bring peace, power, victory, light, life, and liberty to the soul. This is what is needed to save—a righteousness that can do all these things.

Now here is the gospel. The gospel not only announces the sinner's need, it tells of God's provision to meet that need. The gospel message is that our need for righteousness can be—and is— met only in and by the Lord Jesus Christ. *Righteousness* is one of the key words of the gospel. If you do not understand it, you do not understand the gospel. It is as important as that. *In Scripture it is used as an equivalent for God's salvation.* Isaiah 51:5 will make that very clear: "My righteousness is near; my salvation is gone forth." There is a parallelism of thought there. "My righteousness is near; my salvation is gone forth." The two words are equivalent. Righteousness is God's salvation.

Righteousness *is also used in Scripture as a proper name of the Lord Jesus Christ.* He is called "the LORD our righteousness" (Jer. 33:16). Put that meaning of the word into our text and see the beauty of its promise. "Blessed are they which do hunger and thirst after *Christ:* for they shall be filled." Would you have a righteousness that satisfies God, silences the devil, stills the conscience, strengthens you and enables you, saves you and liberates you? Then you need Jesus Christ. There is none other who can save. "Neither is there salvation in any other: for there is none other name under heaven given among men, whereby we must be saved" (Acts 4:12). Jesus said, "I am the way. I am the truth. I am the life." He is Jehovah our righteousness, and He alone is able to save.

The word righteousness *is also used to indicate God's method of bringing sinners into a right standing with Him.* "He hath made him to be sin for us, who knew no sin; that we might be made the righteousness of God in him" (II Cor. 5:21). There you have God's way of salvation with its great doctrine of substitution. God placed Christ at the head of His covenant people and said, in effect, "I will visit on the Head the sins of all the body. I will visit upon Christ the iniquity of all who believe on Him. He will bear their punishment. He will stand under the wrath of God for them. The sword of divine judgment will be plunged into Him. His precious blood will flow to purchase eternal salvation. He will fully bear all their legal liability that they may receive all the merit of His perfect righteousness."

Christ put out the fires of wrath for all His people. In all the Old Testament sacrifices the fire consumed the lamb, but, bless God, at Calvary the Lamb consumed the fire. He came forth victorious. There is no more fire and wrath, no more judgment and condemnation, for Jesus paid it all. He purchased eternal salvation. God made Him to be sin for us. Who can plumb the depths of that statement? Commentators say it means, "He made Him a sin offering." I cannot help but think it means something even more explicit. When God made Christ to be sin, He judicially made Him the object of all His hatred and wrath against sin. He treated Him as if our sin were personified in Him. Think of that. Never let anyone tell you there is no hell. If you want to prove there is a hell, just go to Calvary. God made His Son to be sin. He did not personally become a sinner, but all the wrath of a holy God against sin—everything in God that should have moved against us in eternal condemnation—was vented on Jesus Christ. Why did He do it? That we might be made the righteousness of God in Him. Here is God's way of saving sinners. Jesus Christ stood before God justly condemned by the law of God, because He stood in our place. But, praise God, He exhausted all the fury of the law. Jesus paid the full payment of our deliverance, and now every believer in Him stands personally invested with all the merit of His righteousness. Do you see what this is saying? He endured what we deserved in order that we may enjoy what He deserves. That is God's way of saving sinners. That is what Paul called "the righteousness of God without the law" (Rom. 3:21).

Nothing else can satisfy God. That is why in the parable of the marriage feast (Matthew 22) the Lord Jesus taught that the man without a wedding garment was bound and cast into outer darkness. Can you now see why? Seeing that God bankrupted heaven to purchase eternal salvation, that He made His own Son the object of His wrath to provide a garment of spotless righteousness for guilty sinners, do you seriously imagine that a sinner can stand before Him and be accepted when he is clothed in any other garment? Will you bring the filthy rags of your self-righteousness? Will you arrogantly display before God the tattered garment of your church membership and say, "God, look at me; I'm a Baptist, or a Methodist, or a Presbyterian, or an Episcopalian, or a Roman Catholic"? There is a hell for all who dare to make their name a substitute for Jesus Christ. There is a garment of spotless righteousness. There is a ground of acceptance which God respects. There is none other.

As sinners we need righteousness. *Every soul who longs to have a right standing with God, who desires to be clothed in the righteousness of Jesus Christ, will be filled.* However guilty and filthy you may be, whatever your past, your failures, or your corruptions—however close to eternal darkness and everlasting hell you may be—if you honestly desire to be clothed with the righteousness of Christ, you will be satisfied. The need of the soul is met in Jesus Christ. We read the inimitable words of Isaiah 55:1, "Ho, every one that thirsteth." Here is a word from God to stop any sinner on his mad career to a lost eternity. Perhaps you are saying in your heart, "Preacher, I want something better than I have ever had before. I yearn for the freedom and the cleanness of heart, mind, and conscience that God's salvation gives. I long for the peace that comes from knowing that Christ is my righteousness and that God is satisfied with me because He is satisfied with Christ." If this is the language of your soul, then I tell you, "Ho, every one that thirsteth, come ye." That is the invitation. "Come ye."

91

There is full provision in Jesus Christ. Jesus says, "Blessed are they which do hunger and thirst after righteousness: for they shall be filled." God gives with no niggardly hand. There is full acceptance. When God saves a man, he lifts him from the very depths of destruction and depravity to a height that transcends even the station of the angels in heaven. When God saves, He really saves; He fully saves. When He justifies, He clears guilt away forever. He does not hold your past over your head any longer. He never brings it up again. It is put away. It is under the blood. If you have come to Christ but are still labouring under the guilt and shame of your unsaved life, remember, it is not God but the devil who is bringing it to mind. God has put it away. He gives us full acceptance. God looks on a poor sinner who trusts in Jesus exactly as He looks on Jesus Christ Himself. He enfolds him to His bosom exactly as He does Jesus Christ Himself. He is as satisfied with any blood-washed soul as He is satisfied with the One who shed the blood that washed them. He gives us full acceptance.

With that acceptance He gives us full assurance. As sinners we hunger and thirst for a righteousness to satisfy God, to still our conscience, and to silence the devil. Bless God, all those needs are met completely in Him who is called *Jehovah Tsidkenu*, the Lord our righteousness. No *if*, no guilt, no doubt, no fear. That is why Jesus said, "Blessed are they." When you are filled with Christ, you are blessed indeed.

SAINTS HUNGER FOR THE IMPARTATION OF RIGHTEOUSNESS

We hunger not only as sinners for the imputation of righteousness, but as saints for the impartation of righteousness. The apostle John speaks of doing righteousness (I John 2:29; 3:7, 10). Paul commands, "Follow after righteousness, godliness, faith, love, patience, meekness" (I Tim. 6:11). Follow after righteousness. Justification never stands alone. This is wonderfully illustrated for us in I Corinthians 1:30: "Of him are ye in Christ Jesus, who of God is made unto us wisdom, and righteousness, and sanctification, and redemption." Paul places a little particle after the word *righteousness* which yields the meaning "and both righteousness and sanctification." The idea is that the righteousness, or justification, and the sanctification can never be severed. Alford's Greek Testament remarks,

"Observe the *te kai,* implying that in these two (righteousness and sanctification) the Christian life is complete—that they are so joined as to form one whole—our righteousness as well as our sanctification." When God saves a man, He makes him holy and creates within him a desire for holiness. Paul wrote to Titus in chapter 3 verse 14, "Let ours also learn to maintain good works for necessary uses, that they be not unfruitful." There is a constant teaching in the New Testament that people who are saved should be holy and should be longing to be more and more holy.

As saints we hunger that righteousness may operate in our lives. The saintly Robert Murray M'Cheyne had a prayer expressing the desire of the regenerate heart: "Lord, make me as holy as it is possible for a saved sinner to be." Every Christian, even if he has never used those exact words, has felt that desire. I do not believe in the Christianity of the man who has no desire to be holy. He is a candidate for a hypocrite's hell. That is strong language, but I would rather be strong and true than to use honeyed words that may put your conscience to sleep but damn your soul at the end. When a man has real Christianity, he desires more and more to be like Christ. He hungers; he thirsts. And, bless God, Jesus said he will be filled. Do you want to be holy? Go to the Lord, and He will make you holy. Thirst for Christ. He will fill your thirst. He will slake it and satisfy your soul. This holiness is happiness for a Christian. He is blessed when his longing for holiness is fulfilled.

Holiness is far from happiness for an unconverted man. Paul tells us that the men of this world cannot understand why you are not running to the same excess of riot as they. They do not begin to understand. I remember some conversation I had with the folks in the office where I first went to work. One day one of them asked me, "Do you smoke?" I felt like giving the old-fashioned answer that if God had meant me to smoke He would have made me a chimney, but I politely said, "No, I do not smoke." "Do you drink?" Now, my friend did not mean that literally. She meant did I indulge in alcohol. I said, "No." "Do you gamble?" "No." "Do you go to the dance?" "No." "Do you go to the cinema?" "No." She went down this list of the absolute essentials of life for young people in the western world. She was amazed. "You don't smoke; you don't drink; you don't dance; you don't gamble; you don't go to the cinema. What *do* you do?" Sad! What she was saying was that if you had taken those things out of her life she would have had nothing to live for, nothing to give her

93

happiness. When I sought to tell her that "to me to live is Christ," she did not understand it. To her way of thinking, I was sure to be miserable. Holiness is certainly not happiness to people without Christ.

The opposite is true for God's people. No Christian can be happy without being holy. Christians can never satisfy their needs by simply acquiring things. We live in a society that equates happiness with things—as if you could purchase happiness by buying a new house, or new furniture, or a new car, or better clothes. Happiness does not consist in mere things. No *thing* can make anybody happy, and certainly not a Christian. Holiness is happiness for a believer. That is why God's people can be happy even when they are thrown into vile prisons for their faith. That is why many Scottish Covenanting martyrs took up the theme of the saintly twenty-six-year-old Hugh Mackail. As he was tied to the scaffold to be brutally killed, with a face shining like Stephen's, he cried, "Welcome, God and Father! Welcome, sweet Lord Jesus, the Mediator of the new covenant! Welcome, blessed Spirit of grace, God of all consolation! Welcome, glory! Welcome, eternal life! Welcome, death!" He was truly happy, though his allegiance to Christ cost him his life. "Blessed are they which do hunger and thirst after righteousness: for they shall be filled."

There is such a thing as Christian victory. "Walk in the Spirit, and ye shall not fulfil the lust of the flesh" (Gal. 5:16). Look unto Jesus, and you will run with patience the race that is set before you. "The just shall live by faith" (Rom. 1:17). They do not merely receive salvation by faith; they live out that salvation by faith. They have victory by faith.

> *Holiness by faith in Jesus,*
> *Not by effort of mine own;*
> *Sin's dominion crushed and broken*
> *By the power of grace alone.*

As saints we hunger and thirst after the impartation of righteousness, and we shall be filled.

Servants Hunger for the Demonstration of Righteousness

The word *righteousness* is used in Scripture to mean God's moving to vindicate His truth and His people against all their foes. In Isaiah 46:13

there is a wonderful statement: "I bring near my righteousness; it shall not be far off, and my salvation shall not tarry: and I will place salvation in Zion for Israel my glory." What is the Lord talking about here? Prophetically, He is anticipating the final restoration of Israel. Spiritually, He is describing revival. When the Lord brings near His righteousness and demonstrates His salvation, that is revival. Now apply this to the words of the Lord Jesus when He says that those who hunger and thirst after righteousness shall be filled. Clearly, as the servants of God, we ought to hunger and thirst for revival. Can you as a Christian say you are satisfied with the fruits and the results of Christian service today? Are you satisfied with the attitude of the church, or even of your own heart, toward the matter of earnest prayer? Are you satisfied with your knowledge of the power of God? Are you satisfied with the level of divine movings through you? Are you satisfied to see the enemy on the march with humanism marshalling every power of state, of society, and of the media in a constant effort to crush the cause of the gospel? Surely the heart of every servant of God utters the cry of the sixty-eighth Psalm: "Let God arise, let his enemies be scattered." In every true servant's heart there is a hungering, a thirsting, and a yearning for the righteousness of God. Oh, for the salvation of God! Oh, for a mighty revival! Oh, for the opening of the windows of heaven and the pouring out of such a blessing that we will not have room to contain it! That is the desire of God's people.

According to Jesus Christ our Saviour, this hunger for revival is a good and blessed thing, for He promises all who so yearn, "You shall be filled." Isaiah has recorded some precious assurances to those who hunger and thirst for revival. Let us learn to plead them back to God. Let us be found on our knees day by day, insistently pleading these very words, lifting up these very promises. "When the poor and needy seek water, and there is none, and their tongue faileth for thirst, I the LORD will hear them, I the God of Israel will not forsake them. I will open rivers in high places, and fountains in the midst of the valleys: I will make the wilderness a pool of water, and the dry land springs of water" (Isa. 41:17-18). That is revival! Do you hunger? Do you thirst? Are you poor and needy? Then the Lord says, "I will hear you; I will not forsake you." He says further in chapter 44 verse 3, "I will pour water upon him that is thirsty." Here is the promise for God's people today. We need to plead this before God and keep pleading it until we see it fulfilled. We need it for the church; we need it for our homes; we need it for our families. Listen: "I will pour water upon him that is thirsty, and floods upon the dry ground: I will pour my spirit upon thy seed, and my blessing upon thine offspring." What a promise! I am reminded of a scene in one of the great prayer meetings during the Isle of Lewis revival. As God's people wrestled with Him for the spread of revival blessing, one dear brother prayed what would seem to many a most impertinent prayer, but God was in it. It is not polish that moves God. It is His own promise. This man cried, "O God, You have said, 'I will pour water upon him that is thirsty, and floods upon the dry ground.' O God, I challenge You tonight to fulfil Your Word, for if I know my soul, I am thirsty." Even as he prayed, God actually shook that sturdy Lewis cottage, and the fire of revival blazed on across the island.

As servants of God, we must have revival. If we hunger and thirst for it, we shall not be disappointed. Even in this evil day—should we not say, *especially* in this evil day?—we can see our God arise to vindicate His truth and shower forth His righteousness and His salvation.

SOLDIERS HUNGER FOR THE CONSUMMATION OF RIGHTEOUSNESS

The consummation of righteousness is the reign of Him who is called the King of Righteousness. We hunger and thirst for His coming and look forward to the marriage supper of the Lamb, where we will truly "be filled" in the presence of Christ. We look forward to "new heavens and a new earth, wherein dwelleth righteousness" (II Pet. 3:13). From the depths of our heart we echo the prayer of John as he closed his glorious book of Revelation: "Even so, come, Lord Jesus."

We are in a battle down here. The forces of hell are rampant on every hand, but we have not yet plumbed the depths of hellishness that sin can bring. It is not my purpose just now to go into prophetic Scripture. Suffice it to say that the preaching of the gospel of Jesus Christ has long held our nation back from many diabolical horrors, but as the end of the age approaches, the fury of Satan will be all the hotter. He knows that he has but a short time. But, bless God, at the same time He will be working and saving an innumerable company. I do not believe in a gospel of defeat. In the hottest hour of the battle, the gospel will still be proved to be the power of God unto salvation. We have that indestructible confidence. We have even more. We have the assurance that our Saviour is personally going to return in all His glory.

Thus in the midst of the conflict every soldier of the cross cries and yearns and hungers and thirsts for the consummation of righteousness in the coming of Christ. Now we enjoy all the fulness of God's grace and provision in Him. Then it will be even better. In this world God's people hunger and thirst, but then we will be eternally satisfied. "What are these which are arrayed in white robes? and whence came they? . . . These are they which came out of great tribulation, and have washed their robes, and made them white in the blood of the Lamb. Therefore are they before the throne of God, and serve him day and night in his temple: and he that sitteth on the throne shall dwell among them. They shall hunger no more, neither thirst any more" (Rev. 7:13-16). Why are they free from all hunger and thirst? Because the eternal consummation of righteousness has dawned.

What a consummation! Will you be there? Will you have a part in it? I come full circle in this message and tell you simply and honestly that if you have no appetite for Jesus Christ here and now, you will not be there. You will be like the rich man in hell who longed for a drop of water to quench the raging thirst of his tormented soul. When the Lord Jesus delivered the Beatitudes on another occasion He said, "Blessed are ye that hunger now: for ye shall be filled. . . . Woe unto you that are full! for ye shall hunger" (Luke 6:21, 25). You need Christ desperately. Do you feel your need of Him? Do you desire Him? Blessed are they that do hunger and thirst after Christ, who is our righteousness, for they shall be filled. Cry to Him to fill you with His all-sufficient grace. He will save you, satisfy you, sanctify you, and secure you for time and for eternity. You will live forever in the fulness of His grace, feasting on the banquet of God.

CHAPTER EIGHT

The Law and Logic of Love

Blessed are the merciful: for they shall obtain mercy.
Matthew 5:7

The devil is never more dangerous than when he is quoting Scripture in an effort to confuse and corrupt the souls of men. He even dared to do it when he tempted the Son of God Himself. Paul warns us that Satan will often come as an angel of light. Here is the subtlety of the serpent. When he can induce sinners to commit their souls to some diabolical lie while making them believe they are following the Word of God, he has gone far towards procuring their destruction. The devil always needs to be carefully watched, but never more than when he quotes the Bible. Remember that the next time you hear an apostate quoting the Scripture. Ecumenists, rationalists, modernists, Romanists, and cultists do not quote Scripture to give light, but to confuse men. They are emissaries of the devil masquerading as angels of light. The devil is never more dangerous than when quoting Scripture.

Why do I say that in dealing with this text? This verse happens to be one which Satan has long perverted. He has made it a favourite with a group of people whom a great commentator and writer called "merit-mongers"—people who reject the righteousness of God in Jesus Christ, free justification, and salvation on the merits of the blood of the Lamb. Instead they go about seeking to establish their own righteousness, endeavouring by the merit of their own efforts to create a ground of acceptance with God. How lovingly they fasten on to this text! They are taught by the devil to believe that if you do good, if you are kind and generous, especially to the church, you will obtain mercy from God. So far is this from the truth of the text, that if it were true, Christ would have had to say, "Blessed are the merciful: for they shall obtain *justice."* Once you have settled a solid ground of obtaining God's favour, it becomes a matter of justice for Him to give it to you, not a matter of mercy.

The truth is that in our text the Lord Jesus is not telling men that God will save them for doing their best. In fact, He is not really telling men how to get to heaven at all. He has done that. Notice exactly where this verse falls in the Beatitudes, and you will discover what it means. Verse 6 says, "Blessed are they which do hunger and thirst after righteousness: for they shall be filled." Christ and His righteousness are the centre of that text. He is called "the LORD our righteousness." We may justly read that text, "Blessed are they that do hunger and thirst after *Christ and His righteousness:* for they shall be filled." When a man is filled with Jesus Christ, he is saved. When he has received through faith the righteousness of Jesus Christ imputed to him by free grace, he is saved. So verse 6 brings us to the point where the sinner has really been saved. Now verse 7 shows the first result in the Christian's life. A person cannot be saved without results showing in his life. That is a very old-fashioned doctrine. Many preachers despise it, even going so far as to say that repentance does not involve any necessary change of life. It is merely a mental decision to look upon Christ as Saviour. It allows a man to say, "Lord, save me," even though he is deliberately not turning from known sin. Consequently there is no new life to go with it. Such a decision will never save you. "If any man be in Christ, he is a new creature" (II Cor. 5:17). Any man who has not been born again and created again in Christ Jesus as the handiwork of God has no claim to God's salvation. There are remarkable changes when a man is saved, and our text highlights one of them. One of the marks of the natural man, the sinner in his sin, is that he is unmerciful (Rom. 1:31). As soon as a man is saved, he is described by the Lord Jesus as merciful.

We need to define the word *merciful*. Mercy is more than human kindness. Let me define it for you as follows. When the Lord Jesus speaks of a Christian being merciful, He is describing that tenderness of heart whereby he is so moved at the wretched condition of men that he seeks to remove them from their misery and remove their misery from them. He seeks to do them good. It is the tenderness of heart in Christians which responds to the needs of men and women around them, on the strength of which they are impelled by the Lord to do those miserable people good.

Any man who has not such a heart is yet in his sin. That is a sweeping statement, but I will prove it from Scripture. This is not a description of just a few Christians. It is a description of every Christian. When the Lord Jesus speaks of "the merciful," He is speaking of Christians generally—believers, His born-again ones. There are no exceptions. James 2:13 provides my basis for saying that. "He shall have judgment without mercy, that hath shewed no mercy." Do you grasp the significance of this statement? The man who is not merciful, but who is a self-centred, vindictive, revengeful man, will receive no mercy from God. He who is so full of himself and his own comforts and possessions that he cares nothing for the condition, reputation, feelings, or destinies of other men— he who feels nothing, cares nothing, does nothing, and shows no mercy—will have nothing but judgment from God. He will perish. It is by God's mercy that He has saved us (Titus 3:5). If a person receives judgment and not mercy, he is not saved. So being merciful is an essential mark of a believer. It is closely related to Christian love. In fact, I would say it is a very important aspect and a very clear expression of Christian love. In this study we will look at this love of the believer as our Lord describes it here. We may term it **the law and logic of love.** There are three very simple lines of thought for us to pursue.

Biblical Law Is the Foundation of This Text

Read the text carefully and you will find that there are certain basic Biblical laws a Christian cannot possibly overlook. *First, there is the law that you reap what you sow.* "Blessed are the merciful: for they shall obtain mercy." The implication is, "Cursed are the unmerciful, for they shall not obtain mercy." The basic law of the harvest, therefore, is in operation here. As you sow, you reap. Paul took up this theme in Galatians 6. His words are usually applied to people who make no profession of Christ, but it is interesting that he wrote them to professing Christians. "Be not deceived; God is not mocked: for whatsoever a man soweth, that shall he also reap. For he that soweth to his flesh shall of the flesh reap corruption; but he that soweth to the Spirit shall of the Spirit reap life everlasting" (Gal. 6:7-8). There you have the law of the harvest in a nutshell.

It applies to all of us, saved and unsaved. If you are without Jesus Christ, you are sowing the seed of sin. The harvest of sin will undoubtedly follow. How many poor, broken bodies and minds there are all around us, the products of sin. How many poor souls have gone out into the darkness of a lost eternity, reaping the midnight darkness and the fiery torments of hell, because of the sowing of sin.

> *After the sowing of sin is all done,*
> *After the glory of earth has been won,*
> *After the sands of your life have all run,*
> *What will your reaping be?*

Are you one of those who know the vocabulary of grace, who know the Scripture references for various great Biblical truths, who know the facts of the gospel, but who do not know the Saviour? You are yet sowing to the flesh, to the world, and to the devil. What a reaping there is going to be! The law of the harvest applies to every sinner.

Of course it also applies, as Paul makes very clear, to every saint. There are Christians who sow very sparingly in the things of God, and they reap sparingly. We are living in a day of spiritual drought and famine. Churches are seeing little or nothing of the old-time power of God. Why do you think the whole gimmick trade for bolstering church statistics was ever invented? Why do you think the decision mill, pressing for decisions for almost any reason, ever came into existence? Here is the awful truth. These things are a vain attempt to make ourselves believe that the churches are not in the state of spiritual declension in which they actually are. This is a day of spiritual apathy, deadness, and powerlessness. Why? The sowing has been meagre, and therefore the reaping is meagre. The law of the harvest holds good for the church. The church that prays little, weeps little, works little, gives little, expends little energy, and puts forth little effort for God will be blessed very little, if at all.

Another great law evident here is what has been well called *the golden rule of Christian living*. The Lord Jesus set it out in His own words later in this Sermon on the Mount: "All things whatsoever ye would that men should do to you, do ye even so to them: for this is the law and the prophets" (Matt. 7:12). That is exactly what He is teaching here in the words of our text. If you were hungry, would you not wish someone's heart to be so touched with sympathy as to give you food? If you were destitute you would hope that some saint would have enough kindness to clothe you. If you were broken-hearted you would long for a Christian brother to come and weep with you, to pray with you, and to carry you faithfully to God's throne. As you would have men do to you, "do ye even so to them."

There is an even greater rule than that: *you should treat men as God has treated you.* Be merciful. Why? Because God has had mercy on you. Christians should deal with each other on this basis. Ephesians 4:32 tells us, "Be ye kind one to another, tenderhearted, forgiving one another, even as God for Christ's sake hath forgiven you." If Christians would leave their cosy little corners of carnality and start dealing with one another as God has dealt with them, is there anything that could stand in the way of God's church moving into blessing and revival? That was the secret of the early church. They treated each other as God had treated them. The secret of dealing with God's people is not to look for perfection in them, for you will not find it, but to remember how God has dealt with you. Deal with fellow believers that way. Be merciful, and walk in the light of the cross. Never forget that the blood that atoned for your sin did the same for their sin. The Lord Jesus Christ long ago bore and paid for the very thing that you allow to come between you and them. Treat your brethren as your mutual heavenly Father has treated you. Do it for the sake of the Lord Jesus.

Then start dealing with sinners in the same way. The greatest exhibition of mercy in the world is the mercy of God in Jesus Christ. I was poor, and He came and bestowed the riches of grace upon me. I was naked, and He clothed me with the garment of His salvation and the robe of His spotless righteousness. I was hungry, and He gave me the feast of fat things which His grace had provided. I was homeless, and He brought me into the haven of rest, into the place of security. As Solomon said, "He brought me to the banqueting house, and his banner over me was love" (Song of Sol. 2:4). I was a poor, vile, wretched, guilty, hell-deserving sinner, but God, who is rich in mercy, for His great love wherewith He loved me, even when I was dead in sins, quickened me with Christ (Eph. 2:4, 5). If God treated this poor, guilty sinner like that, how ought I to treat other sinners? Saved people should treat others in the way the Lord has treated them. If we were to start dealing with the world of lost sinners in the way that God dealt with us, who can tell what the blessed results would be?

There is a fourth law in our text: *Christians are in this world as servants.* The Lord Jesus Himself said that He "came not to be ministered unto, but to minister" (Matt. 20:28). Here is the very essence of Christian living. Where there is no pouring out of the self, no consecration of the life, no giving over of our being to God for the work of the gospel, I doubt if there is any Christianity at all. The ministry of mercy is not an option to God's people. It is an essential expression of the very purpose for which the Lord saved us. Jesus said, "I came to serve." That is what it is to be a Christian.

A fifth law to be seen in our text is this: *A wrong relationship with men will hinder a right relationship with God.* "Blessed are the merciful: for they shall obtain mercy." If a man's heart is hardened, he cannot pray. At the throne of grace we apply for mercy (Heb. 4:16), and the unmerciful will not obtain mercy. When a man's heart becomes hardened, that man has lost out with God. Here, then, is the Biblical law that lies at the foundation of this text.

BIBLICAL LOVE IS THE MOTIVATION OF THIS TEXT

I have defined this mercy as tenderness of heart in a Christian, a tenderness of heart that moves and motivates him when he sees the wretched need of men and women around him. A Christian's heart should be soft in the hand of God. When a man becomes hard of heart, he is far from the Lord. The old Puritans used to speak about a melting of heart. That is a very good way to put it. When you draw near to the Lord, your heart is bound to be made tender. This is the heart of the merciful man. He is moved at the misery of suffering souls, and he seeks to help and relieve them.

First, he is moved by the spiritual condition of sinners. Augustine made a very acute observation: "If I weep for that body from whom the soul is departed, how much more should I weep for that soul from whom God hath departed." If our tears flow when we look upon a corpse, how much more should our pity be stirred when we look out upon souls that are dead in trespasses and sins—souls in which the prince of the power of the air is now working, that spirit who is working in all the children of

104

disobedience. It is said of the Lord Jesus Christ, "When he saw the multitudes, he was moved with compassion on them, because they fainted, and were scattered abroad, as sheep having no shepherd" (Matt. 9:36). A crowd always affected Jesus Christ. When He looked out on that sea of humanity His heart was moved with compassion, because He saw them as they really were, not as religious Jews, not as people who were simply hanging on His every word, but as sheep lost and scattered, a prey to the devil, on their way to destruction, and without a shepherd. They had no one to save them, and His heart was tender toward them.

That is what it is to be merciful. When Paul exhorted the Roman believers to reach the Jews for Christ, he noted that it could be done only by the exercise of Christian mercy: "That through your mercy they also may obtain mercy" (Rom. 11:31).

> *Rescue the perishing, care for the dying,*
> *Snatch them in pity from sin and the grave;*
> *Weep o'er the erring one, lift up the fallen,*
> *Tell them of Jesus, the mighty to save.*

Christian, have mercy on the souls of men! Weep over them in the place of prayer. Warn them of their sin, for a faithful witness delivers souls. Witness to them of the grace and power of Jesus Christ—"Tell them of Jesus, the mighty to save." Win them to the Lord Jesus. Have mercy on souls. A Christian, then, is moved at the spiritual need of lost men.

He is also moved by the physical needs of men. Some people see no other needs than the physical. Such are the social gospellers. The major churches that make up the ecumenical movement are full of them. They spend much time on famine relief and various other things, but they have no soul-saving gospel to bring. Their interest and concern for men never seem to transcend this world. The words of John Brown of Haddington are very appropriate. He said, "There is something monstrously absurd in men's being so exceedingly concerned about the removal of the sufferings of a few years, and altogether careless of the prevention of the intolerable miseries of eternity." He was right. It is monstrous, not merciful, for men to spend all their efforts alleviating physical sufferings for a passing moment and to have no time to spend on saving souls from hell. People who do that only witness that they do not believe the gospel or the great reality of heaven and hell.

However, I must also say that it is monstrous for God's people to profess to herald the message of the love of Christ to a needy world and yet remain indifferent to the physical wants of the poor. Christians are not to be hard-hearted about such things. I believe that the Christian church is largely ignoring the poor. How different it is from the New Testament church! The New Testament church was no smug social gathering of the middle class. That is what too many churches have become. I wonder how many of our churches could honestly summarize their ministry as Jesus did His: "The poor have the gospel preached to them." Have they? Oh, yes! We have a rescue mission in town. Thank God for it. I am not to be understood for one moment as raising any question about the good work those men are doing. Thank God for them. But it is too easy to say that we have a rescue mission in town and then sit back like Pontius Pilate, wash our hands, and say, "We have done enough. We give so much a month to the rescue mission, and they do the work." As I say, I praise God for the mission. Our church supports it because we believe in the work it is doing. We send our people down to help them and to witness and preach with them, but the shocking truth is that across this country there are millions of poor people whom Christians have virtually given up. I will be brutally frank. One reason is because of the colour of their skin. A second is because of their status on the social scale. A third is because of political differences. Your political creed tells you, "If they wanted work, they could find it." Are you going to let them go unchecked toward hell for that? Can a Christian sit back and for these carnal reasons justify the gospel not being preached to the poor? Mercy is a scarce commodity among us today.

Thomas Watson, the great Puritan preacher, spoke of the mercy of Christians toward the poor. He noted three elements in it. First, *a judicious consideration*. "Blessed is he that considereth the poor" (Psa. 41:1). Second, *a tender commiseration*. "If thou draw out thy soul to the hungry" (Isa. 58:10). Third, *a liberal contribution*. "If there be among you a poor man of one of thy brethren within any of thy gates in thy land which the LORD thy God giveth thee, thou shalt not harden thine heart, nor shut thine hand from thy poor brother: but thou shalt open thine hand wide unto him, and shalt surely lend him sufficient for his need, in that which he wanteth" (Deut. 15:7-8). Job answered the unjust claim of his critics with the statement, "I delivered the poor that cried, and the fatherless, and him that had none to help him. . . . I was eyes to the blind, and feet was I to the lame. I was a father to the poor: and the cause which I knew not I searched out" (Job 29:12, 15-16). Psalm 112:9 says of the good man, "He hath dispersed, he hath given to the poor."

Love is the motivation of the mercy of our text. When we care for souls, we will do anything that needs to be done to see them saved. When we have the love of Jesus Christ in our hearts, we will give of ourselves and our substance just for the chance to win the lost for Christ. Christians need to be in the place where the only thing that matters is to do what God would have them do to win the lost for Christ—no matter what it costs.

Biblical law is the foundation of our text. Biblical love is the motivation of our text. There is just one further thing to note.

BIBLICAL LOGIC IS THE APPLICATION OF THIS TEXT

Here is the logic I want you to grasp. It is in four simple steps. First, *there is much misery in this sin-cursed world.* It has been very properly called a vale of tears. There is more singing in the world than ever before, but less joy. There is more talk about love, but more hatred. Modern civilization is bleeding to death from a broken heart. Here in the United States there is almost a divorce for every marriage, and we are nearing the time when there will be an abortion for every birth. Add the equally wretched situation in every other country and you will see that there is much misery in the world.

Second, *only Christians have any answer to this misery.* No one else has. Humanitarians may seek to bring relief, but the sad truth is that humanitarianism without Christ produces humanism—and humanism is a foul spring producing only bitter waters that can never satisfy. Physical relief apart from the ennobling message of the gospel of saving grace leads only to more ungodliness and more wretchedness.

Third, *Christians should therefore be full of mercy and use the answer they alone possess to relieve the needs of men.* They are not to be like hermits who have withdrawn from the world. They are not to be far removed from the needs of men. They are to be in the world, though not of it, doing all they can to apply the love of Christ to the needs of men.

The fourth step in the logic of love is that *those who show mercy will be blessed by obtaining it.* They will obtain it from the very service they are performing. "The merciful man doeth good to his own soul: but he that is cruel troubleth his own flesh" (Prov. 11:17). The service of mercy itself makes you blessed. As a Christian you can never be happier than when you are serving the Lord. Not only that, Luke 6:38 teaches that if you are merciful to others, others will be merciful to you in your hour of need: "Give, and it shall be given unto you; good measure, pressed down, and shaken together, and running over, shall men give into your bosom. For with the same measure that ye mete withal it shall be measured to you again." The liberal soul will find in his hour of need that there will be people raised up of God to deal liberally with him. Most of all, God will be merciful to you, for Psalm 18:25 says, "With the merciful thou wilt show thyself merciful." Contrast this with the statement of James that we noted earlier: "He shall have judgment without mercy, that hath shewed no mercy." Our Saviour evidently means His people to take seriously the matter of being merciful.

Here then is the logic of the Scripture—the mind of Christ. We are surrounded by great need. We have the answer. Mercy demands that we put that answer to good use. In doing so we will be blessed by our God and even by men. We are never more like our Lord than when we show mercy.

SOME SEARCHING QUESTIONS

From all this there are two very searching questions that must be put to you. First, *are you in the misery of sin?* Is your heart wretched because you are ungodly, unsaved, unwashed, unregenerate, and unprepared to meet God? You need to be saved. Jesus Christ is able to save. His precious blood can cleanse you. You can be redeemed and go on your way rejoicing in the assurance of sins forgiven. Are you still in the misery of sin? If so, come to Christ. The greatest service I can do you is to bring you to Jesus.

Will you heed the call of the gospel and come in faith to Christ? Bring all the burden of your sin to Him, and He will set you free.

Second, *if you are saved, are you willing to place all at the Lord's disposal to reach needy souls with the gospel?* Will you set your sights on eternal realities? Will you ask the Lord for a burden for the lost? Are you willing to spend and be spent in order to win the lost for Christ?

"Blessed are the merciful." What does that mean to you? It may mean that God is going to call on you to give up something you are hoarding. I suspect, however, that it will mean much more than merely giving money for evangelizing the lost. Perhaps the Lord will touch your heart and say, "There is a world that is lost in sin. There are parts where it is impossible to find a Christian missionary. I want you to go to spend and be spent for Me." Has the Lord spoken to you about your responsibility to apply the gospel of Christ to the situations of great need among men in your own nation or in some foreign place? Then heed His call. With the love of Christ filling your heart, set forth to make Him known to souls who are perishing. "Blessed are the merciful: for they shall obtain mercy."

> Let me burn out for Thee, dear Lord,
> Burn and wear out for Thee;
> Don't let me rust or my life be
> A failure, my God, to Thee.
> Use me and all I have, dear Lord,
> And draw me so close to Thee,
> That I feel the throb of the great heart of God,
> And my life burn out for Thee.

CHAPTER NINE

The Happiness of Holiness

Blessed are the pure in heart: for they shall see God.
Matthew 5:8

W e live in an unclean world—a world, moreover, where men delight and boast in their uncleanness. Even Sodom did not sink any deeper than our modern cities. As in that ancient capital of vice, the men of our day parade their sin with unblushing shamelessness. The riches, resources, and inventiveness of men in the areas of education, art, literature, music, stage, films, science, politics, and business are very largely employed in the spread of mass corruption. From the womb to the tomb men are bombarded with every satanic incentive to give vent to the corruption of their hearts and to follow the dictates of their lusts.

All this is supposed to be freedom. That is the great word of the age. This is freedom. It is paraded as true fulfilment. It is held up as real, uninhibited fun. It is hopelessly old-fashioned to call it all by its proper name—filth. No price seems too high to pay in the pursuit of the freedom, fulfilment, and fun of all this filth. To satisfy the cruel cravings of corrupt men, our jails are crowded and our mental hospitals are overflowing. Liquor and narcotics daily blight their millions and then bury their bodies in a hopeless grave while their sin-sodden souls burn in a hopeless hell. Homes are more like hell than heaven. Children are battered and abused. Abortion mills deceitfully promise to make promiscuity painless by wilfully murdering millions of helpless babies, cruelly burning, poisoning, hacking, or smothering them to death.

This is just part of the price of the life of freedom and fun of this impure age. There are millions of others who have never gone out to live in open debauchery but who fill their hearts and minds with a constant stream of filth under the guise of entertainment. In the secrecy of their hearts and homes they are slaves to habits, passions, indulgences, and iniquities of unmentionable descriptions. They live out their lives with the gnawing guilt of secret sin. Behind many a bland exterior lies a soul in turmoil because of an impure heart.

In the midst of this mad-house of corruption and confusion the Lord Jesus Christ boldly states, "Blessed are the pure in heart: for they shall see God." His words ring out, first of all, in condemnation. Let it be said right away that the standards of Christ and His Word are utterly irreconcilable with the standards of this present age. There must be no trimming of this position by any who profess to believe and hold the Scriptures of truth. In our day, impurity has become so much a way of life that churches are all too often as impure as places our fathers would have called "houses of ill repute." In fact, until quite recently there were worldly associations of men that imposed stricter standards of moral behaviour for membership than many churches do. Nowadays preachers preach on the Lord's Day morning on holiness and proceed to spend the Sabbath afternoon filling their minds with some ungodly film. The "spiritual" ones would never do such a thing—they settle down to watch sports! God help our churches! This impurity is so ingrained that men even try to make the holy Word of God condone it. It is a weak and wicked perversion of Scripture, for the words of Christ condemn impurity.

Despite their clear note of condemnation, the Saviour's words are also words of hope. He says, "Blessed are the pure in heart: for they shall see God." As we shall see, none of us naturally has a pure heart. What we have here, then, is a wonderful promise of saving grace and its effects. It is possible to be pure in heart in the midst of all the evil of this age. That purity will yield true happiness, and that happiness will be crowned with eternal blessedness.

In considering this **happiness of holiness** there are three simple lines of thought for us to follow.

TRUE RELIGION IS A MATTER OF THE HEART

"Blessed are the pure in heart." The Lord Jesus Christ was speaking to people who were fascinated with mere externalism. Their hearts were as black as the darkness of hell. In Matthew 23 the Lord Jesus gives us a picture of the hearts of the most religious segment of Jewish society, the scribes and the Pharisees. They were held by the Jews to be paragons of virtue. The picture painted by the Son of God was very different. According to Him, the hearts of these super-religious people were cesspools of iniquity and hypocrisy. Yet they prided themselves in their religious rites and ceremonies. We read in Mark 7:3-4, "For the Pharisees, and all the Jews, except they wash their hands oft, eat not, holding the tradition of the elders. And when they come from the market, except they wash, they eat not. And many other things there be, which they have received to hold, as the washing of cups, and pots, brasen vessels, and of tables." These were not merely actions taken out of a concern for hygiene. These were religious ceremonies. Religious Jews were punctilious about external observances, but God has placed it on record that though men look on the outward appearance, He looks on the heart (I Sam. 16:7). Job, seeking to answer the question, "How shall a man be just with God?" said, "If I wash myself with snow water, and make my hands never so clean; yet shalt thou plunge me in the ditch, and mine own clothes shall abhor me" (Job 9:30-31). No mere external religious rites and observances can change the wickedness of the hearts of men or satisfy the standards of the law of God.

Yet our churches today are as full as the synagogues of Christ's day with men and women whose only hope of heaven is vain religious observance. They are like the Pharisees of whom we read in Matthew 23. The Lord Jesus said, "Woe unto you, scribes and Pharisees, hypocrites! for ye make clean the outside of the cup and of the platter, but within they are full of extortion and excess. Thou blind Pharisee, cleanse first that which is within the cup and platter, that the outside of them may be clean also. Woe unto you, scribes and Pharisees, hypocrites! for ye are like unto whited sepulchres, which indeed appear beautiful outward, but are within full of dead men's bones, and of all uncleanness. Even so ye also outwardly appear righteous unto men, but within ye are full of hypocrisy and iniquity" (vv. 25-28). Why was the Pharisee "blind"? He paid attention to outward appearance and ignored the inward state of his heart. He prided himself that he was doing what the law demanded to please God, but he missed the spirituality—the true inwardness—of the law.

The sin of vain externalism did not die with the Pharisees. It is alive and well in Romanism and in apostate Protestantism. You will find it even in Evangelicalism and in Fundamentalism. On every hand there are men who have an outward appearance of righteousness. They pay lip service to the Christian religion. They pride themselves in having done what their church requires, whether it is to be baptized in a certain manner, or to walk the aisle, or to make a decision, or to bow their heads and recite the right words at the right time. All such people have is a vain outward appearance while their hearts remain unrenewed. If you have a religion that has left your heart in its state of natural corruption and has never made you a new creature through a living, vital union with Christ, you are yet in your sin and under the wrath and curse of God. You may have religion, but you do not have redemption. You may have the appearance of godliness, but you do not have the reality. It behoves every one of us to find out where he stands in this matter. Every one of us should ask the Lord to turn the searchlight of His Word upon our hearts and bring to our souls the conviction of His Spirit. The empty decisions so beloved of some Fundamental, Bible-believing churches are no more efficacious to the saving of the soul than the baptism of the Romanists, or the rites and ceremonies of those who are in darkest apostasy. Any religion—and it does not matter by what name it goes, Presbyterian, Baptist, Methodist, Episcopal, or whatever you care to term it—that does not purify the heart is not the religion of Jesus Christ. True religion is first of all a matter of the heart.

ONLY THOSE WHO ARE PURE IN HEART HAVE ANY SAVING INTEREST IN CHRIST

"Blessed are the pure in heart: for they [and they alone] shall see God." At first sight *this would appear to condemn all men to a lost eternity,* for the Bible teaches that we all have wicked, impure hearts by nature. Jeremiah 17:9 says, "The heart is deceitful above all things, and desperately wicked: who can know it?" The Lord Jesus testifies in Matthew 15:19, "Out of the heart proceed evil thoughts, murders, adulteries, fornications, thefts, false witness, blasphemies." Notice where He starts. He does not start with your murders and fornications. No, He starts

114

with your evil thoughts. That touches us all. There is no one who can honestly say, "Lord, I am innocent of the great transgression." Of course, the heart produces more than evil thoughts. These seven fruits of a depraved nature are the very things that are committed—and often celebrated—with apparent impunity today. Psychologists and sociologists are wont to put them down to environment and education. They are usually unwilling to face the unpleasant truth of Christ's words. The source of the trouble with men's thoughts and actions is in their nature, in their depraved will. Their hearts are impure. Solomon gives us a plain view of the heart as God sees it: "Who can say, I have made my heart clean, I am pure from my sin?" (Prov. 20:9). Who can say it? The answer is no one, for "there is none righteous, no, not one."

The sentence of the law of God against sin is very plain. Ezekiel tells us, "The soul that sinneth, it shall die" (Ezek. 18:4). Paul testifies in Romans 6:23, "The wages of sin is death." In Revelation 21 we have a final word of warning that impure men will be forever excluded from heaven: "There shall in no wise enter into it any thing that defileth" (v. 27).

By nature we are all condemned, *but God is rich in mercy and mighty to save*. In Hebrews 10:22 He tells us how wicked hearts are purified: "Let us draw near with a true heart in full assurance of faith, having our hearts sprinkled from an evil conscience, and our bodies washed with pure water." The reference is to the Old Testament types and shadows. The sprinkling and the washing refer to the purifying virtue of the blood of Jesus Christ. How are impure hearts made pure? How are condemned hearts saved from condemnation? The answer is by the blood of the Lord Jesus Christ. If you ask, "How is the blood of Christ applied to the heart?" you will find the answer in Acts 15:9: "[God] put no difference between us and them [that is, between Jews and Gentiles], purifying their hearts by faith." That is how sinful hearts are made pure—by faith in Christ and His atoning blood. It is His blood that cleanses. "The blood of Jesus Christ his Son cleanseth us from all sin" (I John 1:7). That blood is applied to the heart by faith: "Whom God hath set forth to be a propitiation through faith in his blood" (Rom. 3:25).

That is how to get your heart clean. By the precious blood of Christ the guilt of sin is removed. Once you have been justified on the merit of Jesus' blood (Rom. 5:9), no power of man or devil can resurrect your sin. God says, "I have blotted out, as a thick cloud, thy transgressions" (Isa. 44:22). He assures His people, "I will forgive their iniquity, and I will remember their sin no more" (Jer. 31:34). It is gone, gone forever, buried in the depths of the sea of God's forgetfulness, covered by the precious blood of Christ. By the blood the guilt of sin is removed.

By the blood the power of sin is broken. Christ not only removes the guilt of sin, He purifies the very springs of your being.

> *He breaks the power of cancelled sin*
> *And sets the prisoner free.*

His Spirit creates a new man. New desires are born within the heart. While Christians are not yet perfect and sinless, they are washed and clean. Jesus said to His disciples, "Ye are clean" (John 13:10). He says the same to every man who has come by faith to receive the cleansing of His blood. The Corinthians had lived in deep wickedness, but when they trusted Christ, Paul testified, "But ye are washed, but ye are sanctified, but ye are justified in the name of the Lord Jesus, and by the Spirit of our God" (I Cor. 6:11). Note the progression of thought. "Ye are washed"—purified, made clean. "Ye are sanctified"—kept clean. "Ye are justified"—pronounced sinless at the judgment bar of God through the imputed righteousness of Christ. That is God's salvation. Though Christians lament their imperfection, they are nonetheless clean.

Furthermore, they love to be holy. There is the mark of a Christian. He loves to be holy. He laments sin and longs to be more holy. A Christian can no more lie down and wallow in sin than a lamb can wallow in the mire. By contrast, though a pig in a modern pen may keep itself clean, it will be content to wallow if the opportunity arises. A lamb can never be content in the mud. There is a picture of a Christian. He is not merely well scrubbed and kept clean because He is in church. He is not holy merely because he is in an environment conducive to holiness and cleanness of life. Any hypocrite with the old pig-like nature of sin can keep his life outwardly clean under the pressure of a clean environment. The Christian hates sin from the inside. He laments his lapses and longs to be more holy. Every Christian can sympathize with the longing of Robert Murray M'Cheyne, the saintly Scottish Presbyterian preacher: "Lord, make me as holy as a saved sinner can be." That is the desire of a man who is saved.

Most of all, the mark of the Christian is that his heart is set on Christ. It is the sincere desire of the believer to serve Christ and to please Him. Robert Murray M'Cheyne expressed it perfectly: "Lord, purify me, and give me strength to dedicate myself, my all, to Thee!" Paul testified for every true believer, "To me to live is Christ" (Phil. 1:21).

This is what it means to be pure in heart—to be washed in the blood of the Lamb by faith and to be renewed in heart to desire His will. Only the pure in heart are blessed. All others are under the curse of our sin-hating God.

THE SUPREME BLESSING OF THE PURE IN HEART IS THAT THEY SHALL SEE GOD

The word *see* means just what it says. They will behold Him with their eyes. They will see God. *There is a sense in which Christians now see God.* This is the vision of faith. We see Him satisfied with the blood of Christ. "We see Jesus . . . crowned with glory and honour" (Heb. 2:9). When we see Jesus at the right hand of God, we see God satisfied by the blood of the Lamb.

Then, we see Him sovereign over all the affairs of men. In the fourth chapter of the book of Revelation we see the vision of the throne and of our God upon it. In the fifth chapter we see the Lamb associated with God the Father upon the throne, opening the sealed book of God's purpose. We recognize when we read those chapters that our God and Saviour is in control of the affairs of men. We worship a sovereign God. I am glad I do not worship any little god who is sitting in the heavens wringing his hands in frustrated goodwill and abject defeat. I am glad we are not worshipping a god who says, "I want to do so much, but those men won't let me. Look at that poor world out of control. I can do nothing about it." Thank God, that is not the God of Scripture! The God of Scripture sits upon the throne. Angels, devils, and men do His will. His counsel shall stand. He will do all His will. We see Him in His sovereignty.

We see Him strengthening His cause and saving His people. He is still saving souls, and He will continue to save souls. We are always hearing about how difficult it is to do the work of God in this secular age. I know it is hard. We can feel it in the very air about us. But God is able to save. He has the same power as He always had. He has simply to speak, and His command is done. I believe in revival. I believe in a God who can answer prayer and send revival. I believe in a God who is going to move by His Spirit and let us see great things. I read in Scripture that the last thing God is going to do as the Lord Jesus comes is to save a multitude. We are told that in the years preceding that event it will be impossible to calculate the numbers of those He saves. There is no room for despondency or defeat. We see the Lord at work in His church.

We also see Him smiting His enemies. I know this is not the language of this ecumenical age. I am glad to be out of line with the spirit of the ecumenical apostasy and to be in line with the Holy Spirit, who inspired David to sing, "Let God arise, let his enemies be scattered" (Psa. 68:1). This divine intervention is something we can experience now as we serve the Lord. The power of God is real. We ought not to be satisfied with a theoretical belief that He is all powerful. We need to grasp the fact that we may see His power at work overthrowing the opposition of men and devils.

Faith's present vision of the Lord is real, *but the great fulfilment of this blessing is yet to be.* "Blessed are the pure in heart: for they shall see God." The essence of heaven is here: "They shall see God." What does it mean? It means to enter into the immediate presence of God and to look upon Him and be accepted, not devoured by the flaming glory of His holiness.

At death the believer passes into His presence. To be "absent from the body" is to be "present with the Lord" (II Cor. 5:8). There, in spiritual fellowship, the redeemed see God.

At the resurrection believers will see God. Job stated the Christian's confidence: "I know that my redeemer liveth, and that he shall stand at the latter day upon the earth: and though after my skin worms destroy this body, yet in my flesh shall I see God: whom I shall see for myself, and mine eyes shall behold, and not another" (Job 19:25-28). Is that not a wonderful testimony and a glorious prospect? I know that my Redeemer, who died on Calvary, who rose again the third day, who ascended to the right hand of God, who currently intercedes before God's throne for me, whose precious blood has justified, sanctified, and purified me, is coming back again, and I shall see Him! Even if this old body has been buried, and the worms have fattened themselves on this skin, and all this earthly frame has gone back to the elements from which it was taken, yet by an act of God it will be reconstituted, and "in my flesh shall I see God." That is the blessing of the pure in heart. Throughout eternity we will dwell in His presence, fully satisfied with the vision of His glory. "Blessed are the pure in heart: for they shall see God."

From that glorious presence of God every unwashed, impure soul will be excluded. Without holiness no man shall see the Lord (Heb. 12:14). Oh, sinners will see Him in the coming of Christ: "And I saw a great white throne, and him that sat on it, from whose face the earth and the heaven fled away; and there was found no place for them. And I saw the dead, small and great, stand before God; and the books were opened: and another book was opened, which is the book of life: and the dead were judged out of those things which were written in the books, according to their works. And the sea gave up the dead which were in it; and death and hell delivered up the dead which were in them: and they were judged every man according to their works. And death and hell were cast into the lake of fire. This is the second death. And whosoever was not found written in the book of life was cast into the lake of fire" (Rev. 20:11-15). They will be destroyed in the endless torments of the never-abating wrath of God in hell. That is where sin leads.

The world says, "Blessed are the impure in heart." That is the message of this age. It is the message of much of its entertainment and art. Impurity is paraded as real life, but never forget that it leads to certain death. "The fearful, and unbelieving, and the abominable, and murderers, and whoremongers, and sorcerers, and idolaters, and all liars, shall have their part in the lake which burneth with fire and brimstone: which is the second death" (Rev. 21:8). Sin leads to hell.

While such men are tormented, at that very same moment, other men who were just as wicked by nature and practice will be enjoying the glories of heaven through the cleansing power of the blood of the Lamb. In Luke chapter 16 the Lord Jesus told a very familiar story. There were two men. They both lived. One lived life to the full, as the world would say, but he knew not God or His Christ. He was unclean. The other lived, or some would say, existed. But he was right with God. They both lived. They both died, for "it is appointed unto men once to die." And they both lived after death in God's eternity, one in heaven and one in hell, one in glory and the other in torments. Between them there was a great gulf fixed. Despite what Rome and certain cults would try to make you believe, death spells the end of all hope of being saved. There is no hope for you to be saved after you die. Luke 16 has a solemn word for us all. We live. We are inevitably going to die. Then every one of us will enter one of those two places with the impassable gulf between them. We will forever be in heaven or in hell. Let me ask you, "Where will you be in eternity?" Your sinful heart will lead you to a lost eternity. The gospel is that there is power in the blood of Christ to cleanse you and save you. My closing word to you would be the word given to Naaman the leper: "Wash, and be clean." Jesus said, "Blessed are the pure in heart: for they shall see God."

CHAPTER TEN

God's Peacemakers

*Blessed are the peacemakers: for they shall be
called the children of God.*
Matthew 5:9

P aul's words in II Corinthians 5:18-21 furnish us with an inspired
exposition of the Lord Jesus Christ's blessing on the peacemakers:
"All things are of God, who hath reconciled us to himself by Jesus
Christ, and hath given to us the ministry of reconciliation; to wit, that God
was in Christ, reconciling the world unto himself, not imputing their
trespasses unto them; and hath committed unto us the word of reconciliation. Now then we are ambassadors for Christ, as though God did beseech
you by us: we pray you in Christ's stead, be ye reconciled to God. For he
hath made him to be sin for us, who knew no sin; that we might be made
the righteousness of God in him."

It is a great blessing to have this inspired exposition of Christ's
statement, because it has been grossly perverted, especially in the last
generation, to present a message which is utterly foreign to the gospel.
Paul explains the meaning of our text with admirable fulness. He speaks
of three things.

First, there are *the makers of peace*. Paul tells us who the peacemakers
really are. It is vitally important to establish their identity. Much dangerous
nonsense has been preached from a misapplication of Christ's words.
According to some people, the peacemakers are the very opposite of those
who faithfully hold to the historic faith of Scripture and are unwilling to
compromise or negotiate on such basic Christian doctrines as the person
and work of Christ or the inspiration and infallibility of Scripture.
Peacemakers, we are told, are the very antithesis of these obscurantist

Fundamentalists. They are, rather, religious compromisers who try to see a little good in everything and everybody, people who are willing to negotiate or redefine every precious truth of the Word of God in order to produce an ecclesiastical harmony. It is unity at the expense of truth. A study of the theological documents agreed on by representatives of the world's major denominations will show that the very heart of the gospel is betrayed to achieve union among the Protestant, Anglican, Orthodox, and Roman Catholic churches. The favourite word of these ecumenists is *koinonia,* fellowship. They want to end the theological controversies of past generations. They are succeeding, but at terrible cost. They give up the faith once delivered to the saints and are hailed as the peacemakers on whom Christ pronounced His blessing.

According to others, the term *peacemakers* should be applied even to those political wheeler-dealers who abandon every principle of right and wrong in order to come to at least a temporary thaw in relations with international thuggery, long enough at any rate for the thugs to ravage a few more countries and push the borders of freedom back even further. Many of the acclaimed peace prize winners of recent years fall into this category. The term *peacemakers* in the vocabulary of Christ has nothing to do with either religious or political compromise. Peacemakers, as Paul makes clear, are workers for Jesus Christ. They are people whose chief interest is to see sinners saved. Their cry to a lost world is, "Be ye reconciled to God. Be at peace with God." A peacemaker is one who is at peace with God, is serving Jesus Christ, and is working to see others brought to the feet of the Redeemer. No one else has a right to this blessing of Christ.

Paul goes on to speak of *the ministry of peace.* What is this ministry of peace? It is reconciliation with God. The glorious privilege of the Christian church is to labour to see men reconciled to their God, from whom they are estranged by sin. Liberals and ecumenists pervert this into a political and social creed. They dwell on what they call the "horizontal" aspect of reconciliation and use it as an excuse to support self-styled liberation movements around the world. The mission envisaged by today's apostate churches is one of social revolution dressed up as Christian reconciliation. The gospel will certainly produce new attitudes among men, but the ministry of the church is to call lost men to peace with God.

The message of peace is the word of reconciliation. What is that word? Is it the liberals' dogma of the fatherhood of God and brother- hood of men? Is it the notion that God will never let anybody perish, but will ultimately accept people of every creed? That is not the message of reconciliation with which Paul ends his great statement in II Corinthians 5. God made Christ, who knew no sin, to be sin for us, in order that we might be made the righteousness of God in Him. This is the message of substitution. It is the message of blood atonement. It is the message of Christ's death on Calvary's cross to satisfy divine justice, put away divine wrath, and save sinners from a lost eternity. That is the message, and it is the only message.

Here then is Paul's commentary on the peacemakers. As to their identity, they are servants of Christ. Their ministry is to call men to be reconciled to God through Jesus Christ. Their message is the blood atonement. This inspired exposition enables us to go right to the heart of our text and to understand the Saviour's message as He speaks about **the blessed ministry of reconciliation.** He says, "Blessed are the peace- makers: for they shall be called the children [or the sons] of God."

THE NEED FOR THE MINISTRY OF RECONCILIATION

There is a great need for this ministry of reconciliation. The world is in terrible condition. In Titus 3:3 Paul exposes the horrible state of men without Christ: "For we ourselves also were sometimes foolish, disobe- dient, deceived, serving divers lusts and pleasures, living in malice and envy, hateful, and hating one another." There you have a very brief but clear word picture of the world as it is today—a world full of filth and folly, a world full of lust and disobedience, a world full of envy and malice, a world full of people who are hateful in themselves and are full of hatred to other people. That is God's description of the present state of this old world. The cause of this dreadful state is found in Romans 8:7: "The carnal mind is enmity against God." Why are men hateful? Why do they hate one another? Why is there division? Why are there wars and rumours of wars?

"Because the carnal mind is enmity against God: for it is not subject to the law of God, neither indeed can be." Men are not at peace with God, and therefore they are not at peace with themselves. They are in conflict with themselves and with those around them. The prophet Isaiah summed up the state of the natural world very well: "But the wicked are like the troubled sea, when it cannot rest, whose waters cast up mire and dirt. There is no peace, saith my God, to the wicked" (Isa. 57:20-21). Here is God's picture of the world as it is today, and He makes the reason for it very clear in a parallel passage in Isaiah 48:18: "O that thou hadst hearkened to my commandments! then had thy peace been as a river, and thy righteousness as the waves of the sea." Do you see what He says? "If only you had hearkened, if only you had listened to the Word of God! If you were in fellowship with God, your peace would be like a river." We sometimes sing the words, "Peace like a river is flooding my soul, since Christ my Saviour maketh me whole." That is a very Scriptural sentiment. Had you obeyed God, your peace would be like a river, ever flowing, reaching into every part of your life and experience. But, "There is no peace, saith the LORD, unto the wicked" (Isa. 48:22). Disobedient, lustful, malicious, hateful, and hating—the wicked have no peace with God, no peace within, and no peace with those around them. How could men ever have peace of heart while they remain in sin? How could they ever be truly at peace with anybody? How can a man have peace when he numbers God among his enemies? How can a man have peace when the wrath of God is suspended over his head and there is but a heartbeat between him and a lost eternity? How can a man have peace when Satan is his master and sin is his delight? How can a man have peace when he is not at peace with God? It is impossible. The great need of the hour, therefore, is a ministry of reconciliation. We do not need new religious programmes, or psychological appeals to some imagined latent potential within man, or some novel social scheme, or political action. The need of the hour is a crusade across the country and across the world with the ministry of reconciliation. It is only when men get right with God that they will have peace in their hearts and peace with their fellow men. That is the need. God says that to us is committed this ministry of reconciliation. It is committed to us in order that we may bring the gospel to a world of lost, restless, needy souls. Every time you look at the ocean, as its tides ebb and flow, as you see the heaving waves, remember, God says that is the picture of the soul of every man without Christ. He is like the troubled sea. There is a constant heaving within his breast. He can never enjoy true peace while he remains without Christ. He needs the ministry of reconciliation.

THE ONLY MEANS OF MEETING THE NEED

The ministry of reconciliation can be carried on in only one way, and that is by the preaching of the gospel. Our text says, "Blessed are the peacemakers." Paul tells us what that means. It means calling men to be reconciled to God. In other words, this text of the Saviour's is a clarion call for an assault upon the gates of hell and the strongholds of sin with the message of the gospel.

The gospel of Jesus Christ is a message of peace, peace in a troubled world. When the Lord Jesus Christ was born in Bethlehem of Judæa, angels sounded out the message, "Glory to God in the highest, and on earth peace, good will toward men" (Luke 2:14). The gospel, then, is a message of peace. The apostle Paul expounded this theme in Colossians 1:20: "Having made peace through the blood of his cross, by him to reconcile all things unto himself." Notice how Christ made peace—"through the blood of his cross." In Romans 5:1 we are told how we enter into that peace: "Therefore being justified by faith, we have peace with God through our Lord Jesus Christ." The gospel of Jesus Christ is God's message of peace, and therefore it is the message to take to sinners.

The gospel places its primary emphasis on Christ, *the Prince of Peace*. Jesus Christ is the gospel. It worries me immensely that in our day the gospel is a message that so often omits Jesus Christ entirely. There is something sadly wrong with a gospel which is full of what men must do, and what men can do, and precious little, if anything, of what Christ has done, is doing, and will do. Jesus Christ is the gospel. He is not part of the gospel. He is not a particular aspect of the gospel. He *is* the gospel. Paul says, "We preach Christ." I am not preaching about Christ; I am preaching Christ. He is not just a point in a message; He is the substance of the entire message. He is not merely an onlooker in the drama of redemption; He is the Redeemer. God's salvation is in a Person, not in a plan. Assuredly, there

125

is a plan of salvation, in which there is a very logical order of events. But no one ever got to heaven by following a plan. It is a Person who saves, a vital, living Person—God manifested in the flesh, Jesus Christ, the Prince of Peace. You will never have peace until you have Christ as your Saviour and He is a vital, personal reality in your life. Jesus Christ, the Prince of Peace! Oh, to get back to the preaching of Christ! When I say that our text is a clarion call to crusade against sin, I am saying it is a call to go across the world preaching Jesus Christ. Go to the rich and the poor and tell them of Jesus the mighty to save. Go to every corner of the world and wherever you meet men—be they black, or white, or yellow, or brown, religious or irreligious, literate or illiterate—tell them of Jesus, Jesus only. He is the Prince of Peace.

Of course, when you preach Christ, you must preach the blood of Christ. That is *the price of peace*. He "made peace through the blood of his cross." At the heart of the gospel of Jesus Christ is the blood of the Lamb. There is no preaching of Christ without preaching His substitutionary, atoning death. It is not preaching Christ to speak in glowing terms about His lovely life and His wonderful compassion without expounding His sacrifice for sin on the cross. It is not preaching Christ to leave men to conclude that they can be saved by seeking to follow the example of Jesus. That is a message of perdition. There is no surer way to condemnation than to parade your good works before God and say, "Lord, see how I have followed the example of Christ." When you place your life alongside that of the Saviour, you will see just how vile, black, rotten, and damnable—I use that word advisedly—every particle of your life has been. "It is the blood that maketh an atonement for the soul" (Lev. 17:11).

It is through the blood of the cross that God reconciles sinners unto Himself. It is the blood that redeems. It is the blood that is the ground of our justification. It is the blood that procured our reconciliation. It is the blood that provides our access to God. It is the blood that gives us an entry into heaven. Without the blood we must perish in hell, but, thank God, there is power in the blood of the Lamb. That is the message. You can confidently go anywhere preaching the power of Jesus' blood. You need fear no imp of hell or shrink from assaulting any stronghold of sin when you know the power of the blood of the Lamb. I would to God that our preachers would get back to it. I would to God that our churches would get back to this message. There was a day when every evangelical pulpit resounded with the message of the blood of Jesus Christ. Great evangelists travelled the world preaching ruin by the fall, redemption by the blood, and regeneration by the Spirit. They never tired of preaching those three points. It did not matter what their text was—that was their message, and they turned the world upside down. That is still the only message. We often sing the words, "Have you been to Jesus for the cleansing power? Are you washed in the blood of the Lamb?" That is a good question, the most important question a man can ever face: "Are you washed in the blood of the Lamb?" Unless you are washed in that blood, you are not at peace with God. My message to you is Christ crucified. I call you to the cross and plead with you to be reconciled to God.

As well as declaring the Prince of peace, and the price of peace, the Bible shows us *the path to peace*. There is only one way to Jesus Christ, and that is by faith. "Therefore being justified by faith, we have peace with God" (Rom. 5:1). Faith in Christ precedes any enjoyment of peace with God. Faith brings a man to an end of himself, to the place where he sees that Jesus Christ alone is able to save and where he accepts the promise of the gospel. He places his trust in the merits of Christ alone. There is a simple acrostic on the word *faith* that will make clear the path to peace: Forsaking All I Trust Him. Forsaking all—all my works, all my merits, all my efforts, all my self-righteousness; forsaking all—all my sins, everything that would hold me back from Christ; forsaking all I trust Him. That is the way to peace. If you have a burden of sin upon your heart, if your soul is troubled, you can find peace at the cross. It has been my joy to kneel with people with shattered lives and broken hearts and see them find peace at the feet of Jesus.

Oh, that you would come to Christ! There is no other way. Jesus says, "Blessed are the peacemakers." Blessed are those who call you to peace with God through the blood of His Son. By inference Christ says, "Cursed are those who do not make peace." Any other way is a delusion. You can find plenty of people to tell you some other alleged way to be saved and to get to heaven. Every sect in Christendom will tell you how to obtain salvation on terms other than these. I am reminded of the words of

Jeremiah: "They have healed also the hurt of the daughter of my people slightly, saying, Peace, peace; when there is no peace" (Jer. 6:14). Bible preachers are often counted hard-hearted because they condemn sin, call for repentance, and warn of hell. Often they are told, "You are not loving!" I can never understand that kind of logic, that it is loving and peaceable to see a man going down to hell and refuse to tell him the truth by which alone he can be saved. That does not seem much like love to me. If your house were on fire, and you were asleep, you would not blame a rescuer for lack of love if he rushed into your room, shook you unceremoniously, and said, "This place is on fire! Get up and get out!" That would not be lack of love; that would be common sense. That is exactly the way it is in the field of gospel preaching. Plain Bible preaching is the best evidence of love for your soul a preacher can exhibit. The liberals have their honeyed words and a bloodless religion to suit everybody. They constantly cry, "Peace," and there is no peace, for until a man's sin is dealt with, until the guilt is rolled away, until the blood has been applied and Christ comes to reign within his heart, he can have no peace. He is still an enemy of God, a rebel against his Maker.

Bless God, when Christ comes in, He brings peace. What peace it is! Peace with God. Do you know anything about this? Can you say by faith, "The sword of divine vengeance will never be plunged into me, because it was plunged into Christ for me; the fire of divine wrath will never kindle on me, for it blazed in Christ for me"? What a glorious thing it is to have peace with God and to know that God is at peace with you. Then there is no enmity, no ground of condemnation. God will never move in wrath against your soul. He has covered you with the righteousness of Christ and accepted you in the person of His beloved Son, so that He could as soon reject Christ as He could reject you, a blood-washed believer in Christ. That is real peace, peace with God.

Such an assurance produces peace of conscience. Paul spoke in Hebrews 10:22 of having our hearts cleansed from an evil conscience. Your conscience is at rest when you know your sin is forgiven and your guilt is removed. God does something that I cannot understand when He forgives sin. He says, "I will also forget. I will never remember your sins against you forever." Our conscience can be at rest when we know that the very remembrance of our sin has been blotted out of the mind of God by the atoning blood of His Son.

People at peace with God and with themselves will also enjoy peace with men. Christians are the most peaceable people on earth. They have not always been given the credit for that, but nevertheless they are the most peaceable people on earth. We are told in Hebrews 12:14 to follow peace with all men. In Romans 12:18 we are exhorted, if it be possible, as much as in us lies, to live at peace with all men. I repeat, the church of Jesus Christ is the most peaceable assembly of people on earth. Sometimes alien spirits get in among God's people, and sometimes even born-again Christians are waylaid by the devil and become factious and bring discord into the church. According to Ephesians 4:3, Christians ought to be always "endeavouring to keep the unity of the Spirit in the bond of peace." Peace is the bond of the people of God. It holds them together as they serve their common Lord. There is peace for the Christian. He is at peace with God; he is at peace with himself; he is at peace with men; he is at peace in the church. That is the fruit of the ministry of reconciliation effected through the preaching of the gospel. The ministry of reconciliation is urgently needed. It can be carried on only by the preaching of the gospel. There is one final truth to note.

THE ONLY INSTRUMENTS IN THIS MINISTRY

This gospel of peace can be preached only by the sons of God. "Blessed are the peacemakers: for they shall be called the children of God." Jesus does not say that because of their peacemaking they shall be *made* the sons of God. No, they shall be *called* or *recognized as* the sons of God. Paul says in II Corinthians 5:18 that God "hath given to us the ministry of reconciliation." At the end of verse 19 he says that He "hath committed unto us [literally, He hath put in us] the word of reconciliation." The gospel is committed to the sons of God, sinners saved by grace. This is an amazing thing. God could have sent angels to preach, but He sent men. The book of the Acts of the Apostles records the story of the conversion of Cornelius. Cornelius was a very devout man, probably a Jewish proselyte, and he was longing for the full revelation of the truth of God. God sent an angel to him. For what purpose? To tell him about Jesus

Christ? No! To preach the gospel to him? No! The only thing the angel told him was, "Send for Peter. Send for the preacher, and he will tell you words whereby you will be saved." Do you see the emphasis God is placing upon the preacher? We have this treasure, Paul tells us, in earthen vessels. God has not given it to angels. He has given it to converted sinners. He has given it to the sons of God. What a privilege it is, then, to preach the gospel. What a joy and a blessing it is that God entrusts to you and me the ministry of leading men to peace with Him. Samuel Rutherford, one of Scotland's greatest theologians, jurists, and preachers, and one of her greatest pastors, was exiled by government decree far from his own church. In the cold north of Scotland he sat in his house and wrote fondly of his ministry in the village of Anwoth, "If one soul from Anwoth meet me at God's right hand, then my heaven will be two heavens in Emmanuel's land."

Let us who have proved the gospel preach the gospel. There is no one better fitted to do it. Christian, God has a ministry of reconciliation for you. There is something in your testimony that God can use to reach some other soul. You may never be a preacher in the accepted sense of the word. You may never be able to stand up before people. You may never have the opportunity to address thousands, but if you are a Christian, you have proved the gospel of peace. As God gives you opportunity, preach that gospel. Tell the world of Jesus, the mighty to save.

If you are not saved, you have heard enough gospel in this message to save a whole world. You have heard enough to save your soul. This gospel meets every need of your soul, and the very fact that it has been preached to you by a sinner saved by grace is a testimony to you that it really works. I am not preaching theories. I am not preaching because it is my job to preach. I am preaching to you because I know whom I have believed. I know the power of the blood of Jesus Christ. I know what it is to be torn asunder by guilt and by restlessness, and to hunt here and there for peace and find none. I know what it is to come exhausted in mind and body to the foot of the cross and to have the sweet gospel message applied to the heart. I know that the gospel works, and I am here as God's witness to you that there is power in the gospel of Christ to bring you into peace. I would finish this meeting in the rôle of the peacemaker. Paul cried, "Be ye reconciled to God."

That is my cry to you. Job 22:21 puts it this way: "Acquaint now thyself with him, and be at peace: thereby good shall come unto thee." What a message! Acquaint yourself with God. Come to know Christ, and you will be at peace. When you are at peace with God through Christ, good—every blessing of the everlasting covenant, every blessing that the precious blood of Christ ever purchased—shall come unto you.

CHAPTER ELEVEN

Faith in the Furnace

Blessed are they which are persecuted for righteousness' sake:
for theirs is the kingdom of heaven.
Matthew 5:10

Christ's blessing and men's cursing fall alike on the same people. You may be tempted to think that someone whose life manifests the spiritual graces which the Lord Jesus mentions in the Beatitudes would be universally admired, acclaimed, and accepted. Nothing could be further from the truth. The Lord Jesus told His disciples not long before His death, "If ye were of the world, the world would love his own: but because ye are not of the world, but I have chosen you out of the world, therefore the world hateth you. Remember the word that I said unto you, The servant is not greater than his lord. If they have persecuted me, they will also persecute you; if they have kept my saying, they will keep yours also" (John 15:19-20).

This hatred of the world is the subject of the eighth Beatitude. Rather, I should say it is part of the subject, because the entire subject is the blessing of Christ upon His people despite the opposition of men—or what I call **the indestructible blessing of the persecuted people of God.** I want to discuss three ideas in the text.

OPPOSITION TO GOD'S PEOPLE

We must remark the total honesty of the Lord Jesus Christ in His dealings with men. There is absolutely no attempt to obtain additions to the number of His disciples by crafty methods. Truthfully He tells them what is involved in being a Christian. He shows them what it is to be a subject of Christ the King. He makes them understand that there is one salvation and one only, and that without it they will face eternal destruction. He makes them understand that if they have this salvation, they will be inveterately opposed and hated by an ungodly world. How different is all this from the ideas and practices of many modern preachers, who appear to be willing to do almost anything to procure a "decision." Their methods are alien to the spirit of the Saviour's dealings with men. They are mere human inventions to hide the preacher's spiritual impotence. When you have the power of the Holy Ghost, you do not need the inventions of men. I have heard of preachers who tell their people how to get "results" when they do door-to-door visitation. They say nothing about really preaching the gospel or about really bringing men to the feet of Jesus Christ. There is not a word about preaching the cross and the atoning blood. Instead there are various gimmicks and psychological techniques to train the mind of the person addressed to respond in a certain way. One preacher is reputed to have instructed his workers somewhat as follows: "Ask questions that produce the answer *yes* and then slip in the question, 'Would you like to be saved?' Before they know it they will have answered yes to this too, and you can lead them in the sinner's prayer." Having said yes to ten or twenty questions in a religious survey, the psychology of the thing is that they will say yes to the next question about wanting to be saved. Great "success" has been claimed for such methods, though how anyone could ever honestly imagine that people will be genuinely won for Christ by such deceit puzzles me. The Lord Jesus Christ worked in a very different way when He was making disciples. He made disciples with an honest presentation of the truth. He placed the issues before His hearers with particular clarity. Here He warns them that if they are going to be His disciples they will suffer persecution.

Christ and His cross can never be separated. The great Puritan preacher Thomas Watson said, "A Christian carries Christ in his heart and the cross upon his shoulder." Martin Luther put the cross right into his definition of a Christian. Describing the word *Christian* he said, *"Christianus quasi crucianus"*—a Christian as if the very word meant "a crucified one." Luther, as usual, did not miss the mark. The Bible promises no exemption from suffering or persecution for the people of God. This has always been the way with God's people. Ambrose, the fourth-century bishop of Milan, said, "There is no Abel but has his Cain." It is always true. The Scripture abounds with examples of this. For an Abel there is always a Cain; for an Isaac, an Ishmael; for a Jacob, an Esau. Paul reviewed the history of the people of God in Hebrews 11:36-38: "And others had trial of cruel mockings and scourgings, yea, moreover of bonds and imprisonment: they were stoned, they were sawn asunder, were tempted, were slain with the sword: they wandered about in sheepskins and goatskins; being destitute, afflicted, tormented; (of whom the world was not worthy:) they wandered in deserts, and in mountains, and in dens and caves of the earth." By the standards of deluded modern Charismatics, these must have been most unspiritual people. They were not rich or at the top of the social scale. They did not experience miracles. They wandered about destitute and afflicted, but they were God's choicest witnesses. Such persecution was not limited to Old Testament times. "Yea, and all that will live godly in Christ Jesus shall suffer persecution" (II Tim. 3:12). Paul assures us that "we must through much tribulation enter into the kingdom of God" (Acts 14:22). The Lord Jesus told His disciples in John 16:33, "In the world ye shall have tribulation." So the people of God are often subject to violent opposition. In the words of our text, they are persecuted.

This word *persecute* is very interesting. Many times it appears with the meaning "to follow," or "to pursue." When the Bible says you are to "seek peace, and ensue it," or pursue it, this is the word it uses. So this is a simple word, an everyday word, that means "to follow hard after." But it came to mean something much more than that. It meant to pursue as a predator would pursue his prey. It came to mean to pursue in the legal sense, to pursue someone so as to bring him into a court of law. It developed to include the idea of vexing, molesting, even hounding unto death. This is the word which our text employs. The people of God will often be persecuted.

All these things I have mentioned—being made the prey of a worldly predator, being made the object of worldly hatred, being hauled into courts of law and dealt with unjustly, being hounded to death—have been heaped on the people of God. They have been the common experience of the Christian church from generation to generation. In John 9 we read of a blind man whom Jesus healed. Would you not imagine that everybody would have been full of joy at what the Lord had done for that man? Would you not think they would have been thrilled to see a blind man given his sight? You would, but you would be wrong, for immediately the Pharisees came and put the healed man out of the synagogue. He at once began to find that there is opposition to any man who will live for God.

As soon as Saul of Tarsus was saved, he was threatened in the city of Damascus. As he boldly proclaimed that Jesus is the Christ, the enemies of the gospel—his erstwhile friends,—decided to murder him, and he had to be let down over the wall in a basket. Through the rest of his life he fulfilled the prophecy of the Lord and proved what great things he had to suffer for Jesus' sake. What a list of sufferings he sets forth in II Corinthians 4: troubles, opposition, persecutions. He takes the same subject up in chapter 11 of II Corinthians: "In labours more abundant, in stripes above measure, in prisons more frequent, in deaths oft. Of the Jews five times received I forty stripes save one. Thrice was I beaten with rods, once was I stoned, thrice I suffered shipwreck, a night and a day I have been in the deep; in journeyings often, in perils of waters, in perils of robbers, in perils by mine own countrymen, in perils by the heathen, in perils in the city, in perils in the wilderness, in perils in the sea, in perils among false brethren; in weariness and painfulness, in watchings often, in hunger and thirst, in fastings often, in cold and nakedness" (vv. 23-27). This is the opposition. It came as soon as Paul was saved. He put it very well in I Corinthians 15:32: "After the manner of men I have fought with beasts at Ephesus." This is the common lot of God's people.

There is a very graphic description of the church of Christ in Song of Solomon 2:2. It is called "the lily among thorns." That is the picture of God's church. It is that special bloom produced by the mighty power of God's grace through the merits of Jesus Christ. But it is surrounded by thorns. Thorns in Scripture are always associated with the curse. Thus Solomon is picturesquely describing man in his sin, opposition, and hatred surrounding the people of God.

The opposition of which the Lord Jesus speaks is carried on in two ways. We will briefly examine both.

One form of this opposition is *persecution by action*. The first three hundred years of the Christian era saw ten officially launched persecutions against the church, the last of them under Diocletian, who was perhaps the most wicked persecutor of all the tormentors of the ancient Christians.

Down through the centuries similar persecution continued. England suffered a brutal attack on the church under the queen who is known in history as Bloody Mary (1553-1558). Many of the choicest saints England ever produced were butchered for their faith in Jesus Christ. In the following century the heather bells of Scotland were stained crimson with the blood of the Covenanting martyrs, men and women who stood for the crown rights of King Jesus and the crown jewels of His gospel. Revelation chapter 17 tells us that the Church of Rome is drunk with the blood of the martyrs of Jesus. It would take a volume even to refer to the various persecutions, stretching right into this century, through which Rome has sought to eliminate the people of God. Add to this the mass murder of Christians by the Communists and you will understand why I say that persecution has continued to be the common experience of the church of God.

For most of us the sword has been sheathed. We should thank God for the power of the gospel. The governments of Great Britain and the United States are not one bit more godly, or one bit more holy, or one bit more interested in the Bible, despite all the politicians who claim to be born again, than those of other countries. The only difference is that countries like the United Kingdom and the United States have for a long time been under the influence of the gospel. We are still feeling the beneficial effects of that. So the sword, at least for the present, has been sheathed. But do not think that the opposition to God and His people has stopped, for it has not. That opposition is always going on. Christians are still hauled before the courts, euphemistically called "the courts of justice." Very often they are courts of anything but justice. Christians in America have been brought before them for such crimes as determining to give their children a Christian education free from the bias of the state religion of secular humanism. One pastor had to stand by while the sheriff forced his way into the parsonage and had all its contents loaded on to a truck and disposed of for defying a state decree to desist from running a church school. In other places Christians suffer job discrimination because of the worldly wisdom of their state legislatures in decreeing the desecration of the Lord's Day. The opposition is still mounting. I am always amazed as I read the news here in the United States. Despite the fact that there are more born-again Christians—and I mean truly born-again Christians—in this country than in any other country in the western world, the meddling by government in the affairs of God's people and the opposition to God's people seem to be worse here than in many places where there are fewer Christians, where the church is weaker, and where the politicians do not even pay lip service to God or His Son. Christians in the United Kingdom have lived under prime ministers who were well nigh communist, and, believe it or not, even they did not do some of the things now being carried out against the church of Jesus Christ in America. Of course, it is going to spread, and if I read my Bible aright, Europe and the Middle East will see the worst examples of persecution in all history.

Another form which opposition to God's people takes is *persecution by word*. Hebrews 11:36 records the cruel mockings which the people of God often endured. In Psalm 55:21 David describes Ahithophel's bitter opposition to him: "The words of his mouth were smoother than butter, but war was in his heart: his words were softer than oil, yet were they drawn swords." In another place he voices his grief at the scorn heaped upon him: "They that sit in the gate speak against me; and I was the song of the drunkards" (Psa. 69:12). David, the man after God's own heart, the greatest king Israel or any other country ever enjoyed, the man who had the signal blessing of God on his life and brought that blessing of God to the nation, was the song of the drunkards. How often this is the case. Persecution by word is sometimes the hardest form of opposition to endure. This war of words never really ceases, and God's people need to be aware of that. If you stand up for Jesus, the world will stand against you. "We wrestle not against flesh and blood, but against principalities, against powers, against the rulers of the darkness of this world, against spiritual wickedness in high places" (Eph. 6:12). Thus Peter warns us, "Beloved, think it not strange concerning the fiery trial which is to try you, as though some strange thing happened unto you" (I Pet. 4:12). Do not be amazed at the verbal abuse—slander, scorn, misrepresentation, and the like—that wicked men will heap upon you because you are a Christian. We must through much tribulation enter into the kingdom of God.

"The friendship of the world is enmity with God" (James 4:4). There is no middle ground with God. When God calls you to salvation, He calls you to a total renunciation of the world, the flesh, and the devil.

He calls you to quit the side of sin and Satan and take your stand openly and unequivocally on the side of Jesus Christ. You at once enlist as a soldier in the army of the cross. I was saved in the Salvation Army. I must confess there are many things about the modern Army that sadden me, but I have to thank God for the spiritual militarism they taught me. I learned that when you came out on the side of Christ you were not called a church member, but a soldier. That is a very good name. From the moment you were saved you understood, "I am in a spiritual battle. I have said farewell to the way of the world. The world is behind me, the cross before me, and there is no turning back."

There is no other way. It is said that Theodore Beza, John Calvin's successor in Geneva, addressed Henry of Navarre—an apparent friend of the Reformation who was soon to become King Henry IV of France—and urged him to throw himself wholeheartedly into the cause of the gospel. Henry's answer was one of the saddest responses to the gospel recorded in history. He told Beza that he would not launch out too far into the deep, so that, if a storm should arise, he might retreat to the shore. That is exactly what he did, and his betrayal of the people of God cost France very dearly. How many Henrys there are nowadays! They make a "decision," or a "commitment." They apparently are on the side of Christ, but in reality they say, "I am not willing to launch too far out into the deep, because if the necessity should arise I want to be able to retrace my way and get back to the safety of acceptance with the world." Like King Henry, they may save their skin, they may save their worldly position, but according to the Lord Jesus Christ they will damn their souls. "For what shall it profit a man, if he shall gain the whole world, and lose his own soul? Or what shall a man give in exchange for his soul? Whosoever therefore shall be ashamed of me and of my words in this adulterous and sinful generation; of him also shall the Son of man be ashamed, when he cometh in the glory of his Father with the holy angels" (Mark 8:36-38).

THE REASON FOR THE OPPOSITION

Jesus teaches in our text that the great cause of this opposition is the gospel of free grace in Christ. Notice this carefully. "Blessed are they which are persecuted for righteousness' sake." What does He mean? What is this righteousness? It is nothing more or less than belief, profession, and performance of the truth as it is in Jesus. Do ungodly men hate all righteousness? Do they hate all mercy? Do they hate all justice? Certainly not. In your dealings with an unsaved man, he would like you to be honest with him. In fact, he would be very happy if you were merciful to him. You will find that the ungodly world likes Christians to show all those characteristics in their dealings among men. But when you bring God into it, that is an altogether different thing. Micah says that what the Lord requires of you is "to do justly, and to love mercy, and to walk humbly with thy God" (Mic. 6:8). Now, if you do justly and love mercy as the world defines those virtues, it will have no trouble with you and you will have no trouble with it. But when you walk humbly with God, that is an altogether different story, because the world first of all hates the gospel of righteousness. It loves a gospel of works. Ever since the time of Cain— in fact, ever since the time Adam and Eve sowed fig leaves for them- selves—men have always loved a gospel of works. They have always reproached and rejected the gospel of the full, free, sovereign, and all- sufficient grace of God in Jesus Christ. They do not like it. They never have liked it, and they never will like it. God will save men throughout the world, but while the devil reigns in the hearts of men, the world will never cease to hate the gospel of God's full and free grace.

If you want to prove that, go out and start preaching the gospel. Start preaching about sin the way the old-time preachers did. Start thundering out the Word of God from Exodus chapter 20. Name sin for what it is. Teach the total and absolute depravity of fallen man. Show him the wickedness of his heart. Expose the foulness of his thoughts and his actions as the natural product of a heart that is rotten to the core. You will find that men do not like it. The most difficult thing in dealing with an alcoholic is to get him to admit that he is an alcoholic. Sinners do not want to be told their true condition. Start preaching against sin, and they do not like it. My unsaved friend, until you see your need and honestly confront that need in the light of God's Word, you cannot be saved. When you feel your need of Christ, you will go to Christ, but not until then.

If men hate the truth of total depravity, what words can describe their attitude to the truth of their total inability to do anything to please God? Charles G. Finney said that men have unlimited ability to bring their souls to regeneration. That kind of preaching pleases men, but if you preach the plain message of Scripture that lays the pride of man in the dust, the world will rise up against you. Tell men that God is sovereign and is working all things according to the counsel of His own will, that according to His grace He chose a people to His name for whom He sent His Son to die, and you will find that they hate this gospel. Paul preached the gospel, and everywhere he preached it people were saved, churches were built, and the devil was defeated. Yet despite all his success he was "slanderously reported" as saying, "Let us do evil, that good may come" (Rom. 3:8). I have heard similar charges. I have heard the accusation that because we preach justification and full acceptance with God apart from any works of ours, we are really saying that personal holiness is unimportant. We are saying no such thing. What we are saying is that holiness is the *result* of God's saving action within us, not the cause. Again, I have heard the slander that anyone who preaches the sovereign, electing purpose of God and Christ's particular redemption of His chosen people cannot believe in prayer or evangelism. The very opposite is the case. I have spent most of my life in the Free Presbyterian Church of Ulster. As a lone voice against modernistic and ecumenical apostasy, we had every man's hand against us. But as we preached, God blessed. As we laboured in prayer, He answered. Today we have some sixty self-supporting churches in Ulster and many more overseas. All of them are the result, by the grace of God, of faithful praying and evangelizing. It is a slander to say that Reformed theology is the foe of revival praying and soul-winning preaching. We expect such slander. Paul suffered it for preaching the same gospel. Psalm 35:11 puts it well: "False witnesses did rise up; they laid to my charge things that I knew not." The sad thing is that so often it is God's people who are engaged in such persecution. A famous American preacher has said that nowadays when he preaches the doctrine of free justification by grace through faith in Jesus Christ, people come to him inquiring what strange new doctrine he is presenting. Many such people, ignorant of the truth and thinking this is a new doctrine, oppose those who preach it. It is always wrong for Christians to oppose the gospel, either through ignorance or through prejudice. Some are so attached to their particular denominational or theological label that they unchurch all who differ from them and end up as opponents of the Word and work of God. Be careful that you do not become a persecutor of God's people under the pretence of your faithfulness to the Lord. Would to God that there were more Christians of the spirit of the godly George Whitefield! Even when John Wesley attacked him, Whitefield pleaded for brotherly love because, whatever their theological differences, they were preaching the same Christ and standing in the same cause. We certainly need more of that spirit today. Let us not be found opponents to the gospel. There is enough opposition from the world in its hatred of the gospel without Christians adding fuel to the fire.

UNALTERABLE BLESSING

No opposition can alter the blessing which God's people possess. Jesus says, "Blessed are they." No *maybe's* or *if's*. "Blessed are they which are persecuted for righteousness' sake: for theirs is the kingdom of heaven." Most commentators take this as a future blessing: "Theirs *will be* the kingdom of heaven." It is very true that all the redeemed are going to heaven, but that is not exactly what Christ is emphasizing here. He says, "Theirs *is* the kingdom of heaven." In other words, the privileges and the blessings of the kingdom of heaven now belong to the people of God. What does that mean? Romans 14:17 supplies the answer: "The kingdom of God is not meat and drink; but righteousness, and peace, and joy in the Holy Ghost." It does not consist in external observances, but in "righteousness, and peace, and joy in the Holy Ghost."

Righteousness: that is justification unto eternal life—acceptance at the judgment bar of God solely on the merits of the blood of the Lamb. This imputed righteousness frees us from the impossible task of establishing a ground of acceptance by our own works to serve the Lord in the liberty of love. Thus justification provides the basis for holy living and victory over sin, as Paul very powerfully argues in Romans chapter 6.

Peace: this is reconciliation with God through the blood of the cross. It brings rest to the heart and leads us into the harmony of the sweetest fellowship on earth, that of kindred souls who have been made partakers of the same grace.

Joy in the Holy Ghost: that is real satisfaction, which is one thing the world does not have. The world has thrills, but no joy. It may have its moments of happiness, all related to circumstantial things, but it has no joy. Only the Holy Ghost can give joy. This satisfaction gives the glorious assurance of knowing, "It is well with my soul; I am ready for heaven."

Jesus says that this is the blessing of His people, even when they are persecuted. Nothing the devil or men can ever say or do can alter one iota the fact that they are blessed of God with all spiritual blessings in heavenly places in Christ Jesus. "Happy art thou, O Israel: who is like unto thee, O people saved by the LORD, the shield of thy help, and who is the sword of thy excellency! and thine enemies shall be found liars unto thee; and thou shalt tread upon their high places" (Deut. 33:29). Is it any wonder that Killian, a seventh-century Irish missionary to Germany, said, "Jesus Christ is dearer to me than all." Gregory of Nazianzen said of Stephen the martyr that every stone cast at him was a precious stone which enriched him and made him shine more brightly in heaven.

How different is the story of the persecutors! Diocletian ravaged churches and razed them to the ground. He commanded Bibles to be burned and Christians to be cast alive into boiling lead. At his word their eyes were gouged out. Their ears were cut off. Their lips were hacked brutally off their faces. They were mutilated and murdered. Diocletian was a persecuting monster. However, despite all his vicious attacks, his victims died with the blessing of Christ and entered into glory, while he ended his days in madness and misery. He poisoned himself and went to a suicide's grave. Charles V, the Holy Roman Emperor, was determined to stamp out the work of Martin Luther. He had a certain captain by the name of Felix who vowed that he would ride up to his spurs in Lutheran blood. In the very night he made this awful boast, he rode into eternity, having hæmorrhaged and literally drowned in his own blood. But even such terrible deaths are not the end for the persecutors. Like the rich man in Luke chapter 16, after death they lift up their eyes in hell, being in torments. Indeed, that is the end of every Christ-rejecter, be he a Diocletian, or a Felix, or merely a person who says, "I will not have this man to reign over me."

Revelation 21:8 is explicit about this matter: "The fearful, and unbelieving, and the abominable, and murderers, and whoremongers, and sorcerers, and idolaters, and all liars, shall have their part in the lake which burneth with fire and brimstone: which is the second death." The first two classes on this list of candidates for the lake of fire are the fearful and the unbelieving. Do you say, "Preacher, I would like to be saved, but like Henry of Navarre I am afraid that persecution may arise. I am afraid to trust and follow Christ." Those who reject Christ out of cowardice are at the top of the list of the condemned. Then come the unbelieving. You may not be a murderer, or an adulterer, or a thief, or a sorcerer, but if you are unbelieving, you are a Christ-rejecter and stand in imminent danger of God's judgment.

The sum of the whole matter is this: indestructible blessing is the portion of every Christian, and inescapable burning is the everlasting destiny of every Christless sinner. Christ is the difference between the bliss of heaven and the burning of hell. If you have Christ, you have everything; if you do not have Christ, you have nothing. That is why Paul said, "But what things were gain to me, those I counted loss for Christ. Yea doubtless, and I count all things but loss for the excellency of the knowledge of Christ Jesus my Lord: for whom I have suffered the loss of all things, and do count them but dung, that I may win Christ, and be found in him, not having mine own righteousness, which is of the law, but that which is through the faith of Christ, the righteousness which is of God by faith" (Phil. 3:7-9).

May God bring you out openly on the side of Christ, whatever opposition it may cause you. Say with Luther, "Here I stand; I can do no other; so help me God, Amen."

Chapter Twelve

The Pain and Pleasure of Serving Christ

Blessed are ye, when men shall revile you, and persecute you, and shall say all manner of evil against you falsely, for my sake. Rejoice, and be exceeding glad: for great is your reward in heaven: for so persecuted they the prophets which were before you.

Matthew 5:11-12

Bible commentators have long debated as to whether there are eight or nine Beatitudes in Matthew chapter 5. There are nine *blessed's,* but most learned commentators believe that we have only eight Beatitudes because they take the words of our text to be a continuation of the idea in verse 10: "Blessed are they which are persecuted for righteousness' sake: for theirs is the kingdom of heaven." However, I believe that there are nine Beatitudes. One thing that distinguishes our text from what precedes it is a very significant change in the wording. Throughout the Beatitudes the Lord Jesus says, "Blessed are the poor in spirit. . . . Blessed are they that mourn. . . . Blessed are the meek. . . . Blessed are they which do hunger and thirst after righteousness. . . . Blessed are the merciful. . . . Blessed are the pure in heart. . . . Blessed are the peacemakers. . . . Blessed are they which are persecuted." All this is in the third person. Now He says, "Blessed are *ye*." The change from the third person to the second is significant. Thus far the Lord Jesus has been dealing with His people in general; now He deals particularly with His disciples who are gathered around Him. We read at the beginning of the chapter, "And seeing the multitudes, he went up into a mountain: and when he was set, his disciples came unto him: and he opened his mouth, and taught them." Obviously a much greater crowd gathered around the Lord Jesus, and He addressed much of the Sermon on the Mount to the larger assembly. But it is very significant that in these verses and in the ones which follow, He addresses the disciples as distinct from the general crowd.

These disciples are His chosen ambassadors, the very people who must soon go out into the world in His name and bear the tidings of His gospel in a very hostile environment. Therefore, with the words of our text, the Saviour takes care and time to speak directly to them about the peculiar burdens which are to be borne by the preachers of the gospel of grace. These words, I believe, have a message for every Christian, but let us not forget that they are directed specifically to those Christians upon whom the Lord places His hand to put them into what we popularly term "full-time service" in the preaching of the Word of God. He says, "Blessed are ye, when men shall revile you, and persecute you, and shall say all manner of evil against you falsely [literally, shall say every wicked word falsely against you], for my sake. Rejoice, and be exceeding glad: for great is your reward in heaven: for so persecuted they the prophets which were before you." One thing is very clear: there is a real price to be paid to be a true preacher of the gospel. There is great dignity in the preaching office. I would to God that preachers would always remember that. It has been well said, "If God has called you to be a preacher, do not stoop to be a king." By His personal call and peculiar promises the Lord Jesus Christ has invested the preaching office with a dignity which we ought ever to keep in mind. But if there is great dignity, there is also great danger. Thomas Watson, the great Puritan divine, once said, "No sooner is any man a minister, than he is a piece of a martyr." The reasons for this are very obvious. A preacher is a standard-bearer for the Lord Jesus Christ and His gospel. Preachers, therefore, need to be kept humble. God humbles every man He calls. As Christ broke the bread before He blessed it to feed the multitude, He breaks the man He intends to use to bless others. Often in a solitude which no one else can penetrate, often in experiences which not the dearest on earth can share, God will break His servants before He blesses them in His service. The apostle Paul was the chief labourer among the apostles. The revelations God gave him surpassed anything known even among the other apostles. Yet, lest he would be puffed up, God gave him a thorn in the flesh, a messenger from Satan to buffet him and keep him humble.

Then, of course, there is another good reason Watson's words were right—that every preacher is at once a piece of a martyr: Satan's malice is particularly directed against preachers of the Word of God. When Syria came up to fight against Israel, her king gave his chariot captains this command: "Fight ye not with small or great, save only with the king of Israel" (II Chr. 18:30). That was good strategy. The Syrians could have slain a hundred better men among the Israelites than King Ahab. It would not have been difficult to find a hundred better men than Ahab. But the battle would have gone on, because with the man who was placed in leadership still in position, the army would have kept fighting. Once Ahab was smitten, however, the whole Israelite effort dried up, and the enemy won the day. The same principle holds true in the cause of Jesus Christ. Every Christian has the devil, his hosts, and his wiles to deal with. Every Christian has his battles to face, but those men who are set apart by God to preach the gospel are special targets of the devil's enmity. If the devil can get hold of the man in the pulpit, he will very often be able to crush the entire effort of the church. That is why the apostle Paul so frequently asked for prayer. He besought the Roman believers to pray for him: "Now I beseech you, brethren, for the Lord Jesus Christ's sake, and for the love of the Spirit, that ye strive together with me in your prayers to God for me" (Rom. 15:30). He pleaded with the Thessalonians in a similar vein: "Finally, brethren, pray for us, that the word of the Lord may have free course, and be glorified, even as it is with you: and that we may be delivered from unreasonable and wicked men: for all men have not faith" (II Thess. 3:1-2). Is this not what we want to see today? Is this not the great burden of Christians as they consider the need of their country? What do we need more than anything else? We need for the Word of God to run across the nation. Too often it seems that the gospel is limping along. We need to see the gospel running at top speed, with mighty, irresistible power. If we are going to see that, we need to have men in our pulpits who are protected by the Holy Spirit as with a wall of fire, men for whom the people pray daily that God will keep His hand upon them and that no shaft from the enemy will penetrate their armour or bring them down to defeat. If Paul needed such prayer support from the people of God, how much more do preachers today!

Though preachers must endure the blast of the devil, they are assured of the blessing of the Lord. Amid the conflict, they have comfort now and the assurance of a crown hereafter. Here, then, are the two sides of the gospel ministry: on the one hand the blasting of the devil's opposition, and on the other hand the blessing of the Lord—what we may call **the pain and the pleasure of preaching Christ in a sinful world.**

ANTAGONISM TO THE GOSPEL

Christ and His gospel—and those who preach it—have always met with antagonism and bitter opposition. A moment's reflection will establish the truth of this observation. Moses was repeatedly reviled. Samuel was rejected by the children of Israel, whom he had delivered from destruction. Elijah, the prophet of fire, was mocked, despised, cursed, and threatened. Micaiah, that faithful man who witnessed to Ahab and Jehoshaphat before they went to battle, was bitterly hated and imprisoned. Jeremiah suffered a conspiracy against his life. He was thrown into a deep, dirty, damp dungeon. He then endured a forced captivity in Egypt until he died. Daniel was thrown into a den of lions. Nehemiah was mocked and oppressed. And so the story goes on through the Old Testament. We turn to the pages of the New Testament. Christ Himself was set at naught of men. He was beaten, He was mocked, He was scourged, and finally He was put to death. His apostles walked the same road. Stephen was stoned. James was beheaded. Peter was thrown into prison. Paul was beaten, stoned, and left for dead. Then, as an old man, after a cruel imprisonment, he was beheaded. In post-apostolic days the church continued to suffer the same opposition.

Through the centuries flows the river of the blood of the saints of God. To this very day it is the same story. In the relative comfort of this land we tend to forget that the twentieth century has been as violent as any against the people of God. Millions have suffered imprisonment or death for their allegiance to Christ. The world has never been the friend of grace, and it never will be. This is an age of corruption and sin, and in every ungodly heart there is an inveterate opposition to Christ and His gospel and to any man who dares to stand for it.

The reasons for this opposition are not difficult to discover. If you read beyond the Beatitudes in Matthew chapter 5, you will find that Jesus says, "Ye are the salt of the earth" (v. 13). Here is the first reason men hate the gospel and those who preach it: *salt has a very strong savour.* So do

Christians who witness for their Lord. It is a savour that ungodly people do not like. Men do not like the preaching of the gospel. They hate the exposition of what this Bible says about sin. They do not wish to be reminded that there is a holy God in heaven and that He has the right to command their obedience and set their standards. They are incensed at any mention of the judgment of God and His everlasting punishment of all who do not know His Son as Saviour. They like God's way of salvation from sin and destruction even less. Talk to them about a fountain filled with blood and it stirs the resentment of their hearts. They would rather hear some man-centred message of their innate goodness and ability to earn eternal life by their supposed good works. The strong savour of the gospel is more than ungodly men can stomach. The apostle Paul said, "For we are unto God a sweet savour of Christ, in them that are saved, and in them that perish: to the one we are the savour of death unto death; and to the other the savour of life unto life. And who is sufficient for these things?" (II Cor. 2:15-16).

Salt has a strong savour. *It also smarts*. It causes men to feel their wounds. That is one purpose of our gospel witness. Men can feel good about themselves until they hear the gospel. I once had a young man whom I had invited to a gospel service tell me why he would not come. He was honest about it and told me he could go to his own church and feel comfortable. In fact, he could settle down behind a pillar and go to sleep. He expressed his fear that if he came to our service he would not be able to sleep through the message, and that if he listened he might hear something that would awaken his conscience. How often that is the case. Men can feel quite good about themselves until they have to face up to the gospel. As long as they measure themselves by others who are equally sinful they can pride themselves on being wonderful people. But when they expose their lives to the light of the Word of God, they discover that they are poor, vile, guilty, hell-deserving sinners. So it is natural that men resent the salty sting of the gospel.

What is more, the gospel is like salt in that *it fights putrefaction*. Clearly, all the forces that have a vested interest in moral decadence will oppose those whose Christian witness threatens them. The liquor barons, the drug lords, the pornography peddlers, the abortion-mongers, and such like have nothing to fear from leftist, liberal churchmen whose preaching is more like an exposition of the Humanist Manifesto than of Scripture. But they do recognize a true gospel witness as a danger to their nefarious devices. That is why their friends in the media and in politics so often caricature and misrepresent God's people. It is simply because they are the real antidote to the nation's moral putrefaction.

A very important principle arises here. Christians are salt. They fight putrefaction. They do so by their gospel witness, not by amalgamation with the very forces the gospel opposes. Some Christians want to fight racism by joining hands with Marxist revolutionaries. That is the official policy of the World Council of Churches, for example, but it is not the policy of Scripture. Others try to fight abortion on demand by merging their efforts with those of the Roman Catholic Church. The description of that church in Revelation chapter 17 precludes any joint effort with her. Rome is part of the putrefaction the gospel combats. We cannot oppose sin by joining hands with sin, but by a faithful gospel witness.

Christ gives a second reason for the world's opposition to His people. He says, "Ye are the light of the world" (v. 14). That is an amazing statement. There is a message here for every Christian, but particularly for every preacher. The only light in this land is going to come from its pulpits. I am in favour of good educational establishments, but they will not dispel the horror of great darkness that lies upon the land. The only light will come from the pulpits.

"Ye are the light of the world." I say this is an amazing statement because Christ said in John 8:12 and in John 9:5, "*I* am the light of the world." How can we reconcile those two statements? Very simply. We have no light but Christ and no message but Christ. As a preacher of Christ, I have the only light that can overcome the darkness of this old world. When Adoniram Judson returned from Burma on furlough, churches were agog with excitement. They had heard of tremendous happenings on the mission field and were impatient to hear Judson tell about his confrontations with heathenism. But the great missionary did not mention anything about where he had been, what he had seen, what he had said, or what he had done. He simply preached to them on the beauty of Christ. A minister complained afterwards to him, "I think the people were disappointed. They expected to hear some of your exciting experiences on the mission field." Judson looked at him and said, "Can you tell me anything more exciting than 'God so loved the world, that he gave his only begotten Son'?" Judson knew that Christ was his only message. That message had wrought great miracles of grace on the mission field, and it was the message his homeland needed just as much as Burma did.

If you preach this light, let me tell you, you will be opposed. In John 1:5 we read, "The light shineth in darkness; and the darkness comprehended it not." The meaning is, "The darkness *overcame* it not." The thought of conflict is inherent in that word. Jesus said, "Light is come into the world, and men loved darkness rather than light, because their deeds were evil" (John 3:19). So when you come preaching the light, men do not welcome it, for they hate the light.

In every age there is antagonism to the gospel and to those who preach it. But, praise God, He has His people to save in every age. Despite this antagonism, the gospel will be successful. We can go to any mission field in the world and be assured that out of every tribe, tongue, kindred, and nation God is going to save a people for His name. When Paul went to Corinth some people were saved, and immediately there was uproar. Then the Lord appeared to Paul in a vision and said, "Be not afraid, but speak, and hold not thy peace: for I am with thee, and no man shall set on thee to hurt thee: for I have much people in this city" (Acts 18:9, 10). In effect, the Lord said, "Paul, you see these wicked Corinthians in their heathenism, hatred, blindness, and sin. But in this heathen city I have many people whom I am going to save." I am glad I believe in a sovereign God who elects His people according to His purpose, a God who has a people to save and who is going to save them however much the devil and his minions may oppose Him. Do not be afraid of the opposition. In this evil age there will always be antagonism to us and our message, but we should be encouraged that the Lord will bless the witness of His people and will infallibly save His people from their sins.

THE FORMS ANTAGONISM TAKES

This antagonism expresses itself in three common forms. The aim in each case is to hinder, to stop, and to nullify the preaching of the gospel. However, there is always an answer to these satanic aims. "The weapons of our warfare are not carnal, but mighty through God to the pulling down of strong holds" (II Cor. 10:4). Let me point out the three forms of attack upon God's people and show you how there is victory for them in every case.

The first attack is on the mind of the Lord's servant. Notice the word *revile*: "Blessed are ye, when men shall revile you," or reproach you. The devil's aim here is to make God's servant feel shame and so render his witness powerless. For example, he may bring up past sins. Every Christian knows something about this. The devil reproaches us over what we did in our unsaved days. He brings up sins from our past and tries to ensure that we can never forget it. Then again, he may reproach us with our failures in the Lord's service. Very few preachers go home content with their preaching. They may be very glad at what the Lord has done and give Him the glory for every blessing He has bestowed, but they feel their inadequacies and failures. Satan may even reproach us for the very stand we take and for the gospel we preach. He may point out that others are not taking the same stand and make us feel very much alone. He will revile us. If he can induce us to accept his slanders, he will have gone a long way toward defeating us in our ministry and silencing our witness.

There is an answer. When the devil reviles you, accept no guilt from him. If you are a Christian, the Lord will convict your heart of the things in your life that need to be put right. Let the Lord do that, but never accept shame or guilt from the devil. When the devil reviles you, you have a ready answer: "I am right with God through the blood of Christ. I am justified freely by the grace of God through the redemption that is in Christ Jesus. The law of God has nothing against me. My sin is buried in the sea of His forgetfulness. It is purged with the precious blood of Christ. I am right with God. I am accepted in Christ." When the devil tries to heap shame upon you, this is the answer. I know there are preachers who tell you to argue with the devil. They even advise you as to what you should say. But why would any Christian wish to carry on a conversation with the devil? The way to deal with the devil is to talk to the Lord. Get alone with Him and praise Him that you are justified through Christ. Let God's Word witness that to your heart.

As far as your stand for God is concerned, use the same argument. In his epistles Paul constantly asserted, "I am an apostle of Jesus Christ. I am an apostle who is called of God. I am an apostle by the will of God." Why did he do that? We are often told that it was because so many people sought to deny his apostleship. There is much truth in that, but there is another very good reason. He says in effect, "God has called me. God has commissioned me. I am right in what I am doing, and there is no man or devil who can make me ashamed of my service." When you are doing the will of God, never allow the devil to shame you. Look unto Jesus. "Consider him ... lest ye be wearied and faint in your minds" (Heb. 12:3).

The second line of attack is on the body of the Lord's servant with the aim of causing suffering and ultimate surrender. That is the significance of the word *persecute*. The devil is always keen to use this weapon, but often it backfires. When the devil inspired Mary Tudor, queen of England, to murder men of God, the plan backfired. No words ever proved truer than the words of Hugh Latimer as he was put to the stake: "Fear not, Master Ridley, for we shall by God's grace light a candle in England this day that shall never be put out." How right he was! The fear of God and the faith of the gospel proved more potent than the fear of physical suffering. The flame of Latimer's witness consumed the fire of Mary's persecution. Paul told the Ephesian elders, "And now, behold, I go bound in the spirit unto Jerusalem, not knowing the things that shall befall me there: save that the Holy Ghost witnesseth in every city, saying that bonds and afflictions abide me. But none of these things move me, neither count I my life dear unto myself, so that I might finish my course with joy, and the ministry, which I have received of the Lord Jesus, to testify the gospel of the grace of God" (Acts 20:22-24). When you know the power of the gospel and when you are sure your soul is ready for heaven, that faith will always make you more than a conqueror through Christ.

The third form of attack on God's people is lying accusation. "They will say every evil word against you falsely." That is aimed at our reputation, and it means to cause us to be silent. False accusations are very difficult to repel. Preachers are especially vulnerable. They need to be extremely careful not to give any opportunity to anyone to question their morality or integrity. Let us each live before God in such purity that we can call Him to witness that any accusation against us is false. Such accusations will come: "They will say every wicked word against you falsely for my sake." Satan, who is the father of every lie, knows that if he can ruin a preacher's reputation he has silenced him.

The answer to false accusation is a holy life. Let us ensure that every evil word spoken against us is false. "For so is the will of God, that with well doing ye may put to silence the ignorance of foolish men" (I Pet. 2:15). That is the answer. Here, then, are the three forms that opposition to the Lord's servants takes: reviling, persecution, and lying accusation. Thomas Watson was right in his statement that as soon as God makes a man a minister—we may even say as soon as God makes a man a Christian—he is at once a piece of a martyr.

OUR COMFORT AND JOY UNDER ATTACK

In the midst of all this antagonism the servant of Jesus Christ has great joy and great comfort. "Blessed are ye, when men shall revile you. . . . Rejoice, and be exceeding glad." The word translated "exceeding glad" indicates spiritual exultation. It is the word used of the Lord Jesus in Luke 10:21: "Jesus rejoiced in spirit." It is the word that Mary used in her great song in Luke 1:47 when she said she rejoiced in God her Saviour. It is the word that is used of Abraham in John 8:56: "Abraham rejoiced to see my day." The man who is called of God and who is willing to live and die by the Bible has this same spiritual exultation in the midst of his conflict with the powers of hell.

First of all, he has the comfort and the joy of *knowing that he is on the Lord's side* and the Lord is on his side. The psalmist rejoiced in this assurance: "God is our refuge and strength, a very present help in trouble. Therefore will not we fear, though the earth be removed, and though the mountains be carried into the midst of the sea; though the waters thereof roar and be troubled, though the mountains shake with the swelling thereof. Selah. There is a river, the streams whereof shall make glad the city of God, the holy place of the tabernacles of the most High. God is in the midst of her; she shall not be moved: God shall help her, and that right early. . . . The LORD of hosts is with us; the God of Jacob is our refuge" (Psa. 46:1-5, 7). Paul says in Romans 8:31, "If God be for us, who can be against us?" It is a great comfort in any conflict to know that we are on the Lord's side.

There is also the joy of *being identified with the greatest men who ever lived.* "Be exceeding glad . . . for so persecuted they the prophets." The implication is clear: "I am putting you among those eminent people." I believe in apostolic succession, but it is a preaching succession. I am in a succession that started at the dawn of time and has continued through every succeeding age with great prophets, great preachers, great apostles, great reformers, great evangelists, and great pastors. Every man who preaches Jesus Christ is in that succession. If you are going to have the world against you, is it not good to know that you are standing where Moses stood, where Elijah stood, where John the Baptist stood, where Paul, Peter, James, John, Andrew, Philip, Bartholomew, and the rest of the apostles stood? That is the crowd I want to be with. I am not ashamed of the prophets of the Lord or of the apostles of the Lord or of the great Reformers and preachers since the New Testament period. I would rather be on that side than line up with the enemies of Christ. Though most unworthy, I am glad to be numbered among the saints of God, washed in the blood of the Lamb, purchased with the redemption of Jesus Christ, blessed in being called to be a preacher of the gospel.

Our third comfort and joy is *the assurance of a great reward.* Rejoice, for this old world is not the end. Paul told the Corinthians, "Judge nothing before the time." The day of our Lord's return is hastening, and just one glimpse of Christ will repay all our suffering.

> *It will be worth it all,*
> *When we see Jesus.*
> *One look at His dear face*
> *All sorrows will erase.*
> *It will be worth it all,*
> *When we see Him.*

His "Well done" will be a great reward, but that will be only the beginning. "Enter thou into the joy of thy Lord" is His welcome to His people—a welcome that holds all the fulness of eternal bliss in His presence. Then

155

we shall have unalloyed joy, unbroken peace, and unending pleasures at His right hand.

The pain of serving Christ is, to use Paul's words, a "light affliction." It endures only "for a moment." The pleasure of serving Christ is something we now experience in the knowledge of the power and presence of the Saviour, and it will last forever in what Paul called the "far more exceeding and eternal weight of glory."

With this in mind, Abraham looked for a city which has foundations, whose builder and maker is God, and faithfully served the Lord. Similarly, Moses repudiated Egypt and chose rather to suffer affliction with the people of God. Because he "had respect unto the recompence of the reward," he "endured, as seeing him who is invisible." Paul expressed the same faith in his famous words, "I press toward the mark for the prize of the high calling of God in Christ Jesus."

There is an urgent need for such dedicated servants of Christ today. Martin Luther was right when he said, "It is not possible to be a faithful preacher and not meet with trials and oppositions." But Paul assures us, "Our sufficiency is of God" (II Cor. 3:5). Therefore with the apostle we can say, "Thanks be unto God, which always causeth us to triumph in Christ, and maketh manifest the savour of his knowledge by us in every place" (II Cor. 2:14).

There is pain in serving Christ. There is also pleasure. The pleasure outweighs the pain now and will replace it entirely throughout the ages of eternity in heaven.

CHAPTER THIRTEEN

Christ's Redemption

Matthew 5:3-12

C hristian character is nothing more or less than Christ-likeness, and despite what some Dispensationalists have said about the Sermon on the Mount, it is Christian character which the Lord Jesus Christ is describing in the Beatitudes and which He so blesses. What we have before us in Matthew 5:1-12 is the picture of a Christian conformed to the image of Jesus Christ. In other words, the Lord Jesus Christ Himself is the great Original of all the virtues and graces which are listed for us in verses 3 through 11. Therefore, in our last two studies we will consider the theme of Christ in the Beatitudes. The portrait is a many-sided one of "the man Christ Jesus," the mediator between God and men, the procurer of every gospel blessing, and the covenant head of those people who are so richly blessed by His provision.

There are two distinct ways of considering Christ in the Beatitudes. First of all, we can do so by concentrating on the commencement of each Beatitude to see a description of His person and work. Second, by concentrating on the promised reward at the end of each Beatitude, we can see what He actually accomplished for His people. In this study we will take the first of these two ways of dealing with Christ in the Beatitudes. Thus our subject is **the person and work of Christ our Saviour as seen in the Beatitudes.** You may recall that I mentioned a dispute among commentators as to whether there are eight or nine Beatitudes. I have adopted the obvious conclusion that since there are nine *"blessed's,"* there are nine Beatitudes. These nine fall into three sets of three, and that is how we are going to treat them. Each of these sets of three has a particular and dominant theme. In the first three Beatitudes our attention is focused upon Christ's humble character. In the second three Beatitudes the emphasis is upon Christ's gracious life. In the third set of Beatitudes the theme is Christ's atoning death. All of these are vital to our salvation and deserve our closest attention.

CHRIST'S HUMBLE CHARACTER

The Lord Jesus Christ plumbed the depths of humiliation in order to save us. That humiliation is eloquently described in the terms used in the first three Beatitudes. Notice that He uses the words "poor in spirit." Then He speaks of those who "mourn," and finally of those who are "meek." Remember that He is the great Original of these graces, and when He is blessing these things in Christians, He is really saying, "If you would understand Him who is truly poor in spirit, if you would come to know Him who truly mourns and Him who is truly meek, then you must come to know Me."

First of all, *He is poor in spirit.* I have pointed out that the particular Greek word that is used here means "desperately poor." It is the deepest kind of poverty that a person may suffer. It is not the word that you would use, for instance, of a working man who is bringing in some money but still does not have enough to live on. This word is the word for that person who has plumbed the deepest depths of poverty. It is the same root word as you find in that great text in II Corinthians 8:9, where Paul said to the Corinthians, "Ye know the grace of our Lord Jesus Christ, that, though he was rich, yet for your sakes he became poor, that ye through his poverty might be rich." This poverty is described for us again by the apostle Paul in Philippians 2:6-8: "[Christ], being in the form of God, thought it not robbery to be equal with God." There has been much scholarly discussion on the meaning of this statement. I take it to mean that Christ's equality with God, this glory, was not something either to be grasped at or held on to. He thought it not robbery to be equal with God, "but made himself of no reputation," or as B. B. Warfield translated it, "He made Himself of no account." How? He "took upon him the form of a servant, and was made in the likeness of men: and being found in fashion as a man, he humbled himself, and became obedient unto death, even the death of the cross." This is the becoming poor that Paul speaks about. Christ the King was born, not in a palace, but in a manger. He lived, not in royal surroundings, but as an itinerant preacher. There is a tremendous pathos in His words in Matthew 8:20: "The foxes have holes, and the birds of the air have nests; but the Son of man hath not where to lay his head." He was buried in a borrowed tomb. In human terms, He plumbed the depths of poverty, but all this only evidenced the deep humility of His holy soul. In Hebrews 12:2 we are commanded to look "unto Jesus the author and finisher of our faith; who for the joy that was set before him endured the cross, despising the shame." Normally this is taken to mean that because of the great reward of joy that was beyond the cross, Christ was willing to endure all His humiliation. That is a very proper, Scriptural doctrine. Personally, however, I do not think that is what the apostle is teaching here. The word *for*— "who for the joy that was set before him"—has the meaning of "instead of." The word that is translated "set before" means literally "to lie before," or "to be present with a person." For instance, when in II Corinthians 8:12 Paul says, "If there be first a willing mind," literally he says, "If readiness is present." It is the same word. Now look again at Hebrews 12:2: "Who *instead of* the joy that was *present before* Him, endured the cross." Here is a glimpse of the great mystery of eternity, when by a decisive act of the divine will the Son of God laid aside the robes of His splendour and, instead of the joy that was His in the glories of heaven, chose to endure all the humiliation of coming to earth, all the agony of going to the cross, in order to save His people from their sin. What condescension to bring us redemption! Rightly did the prophet Zechariah say, "He is just, and having salvation; lowly, and riding upon an ass" (Zech. 9:9). Well did Christ Himself say, "I am meek and lowly in heart" (Matt. 11:29). For the great Creator to take flesh was an act of unspeakable self-humbling. When the Lord Jesus came into the world, He deliberately plumbed the depths of human need so that He could be the Saviour and the sympathizer of men in every station of life, even those in the worst possible condition. Christ was poor in spirit.

Also, *He mourned.* This mourning was especially on account of sin. Who ever felt the horror of sin like the sinless Son of God? You and I are sinners by nature, and we become so used to the sin around us that we can take in our stride things that are absolutely heinous in the sight of God. But try to imagine what it meant for the pure and holy Son of God to come into a world of sin, to be tempted of the devil, and to hear the hiss of the serpent in His ear with every foul insinuation that that hellish mind could devise. Then consider what it must have been like for that sinless Saviour actually to bear our sins in His own body on the tree. No one ever felt the horror of sin like Jesus Christ. Isaiah said of Him, "He is despised and rejected of men; a man of sorrows, and acquainted with grief" (Isa. 53:3). He is the one who mourned. I am glad He plumbed those depths of tears, because we live in a world where everybody can cause a broken heart, but nobody can cure it. We can be the cause of tears, and though we may physically wipe them away, in reality we cannot remove the hurt. Thank God for one who has wept, who knows what sin is, who hates it with a holy hatred, who has conquered it, and who can wipe the tears that it causes from our eyes. Hebrews 4:15 says that He "was in all points tempted like as we are, yet without sin."

> *Is there anyone can help us, one who understands our hearts,*
> *When the thorns of life have pierced them till they bleed;*
> *One who sympathizes with us, who in wondrous love imparts*
> *Just the very, very blessing that we need?*
>
> *Yes, there's One, only One,*
> *The blessed, blessed Jesus, He's the One!*
> *When afflictions press the soul,*
> *When waves of trouble roll,*
> *And you need a friend to help you,*
> *He's the One.*

He was poor in spirit. He felt the horror of sin.

Finally, He was meek. I defined meekness as the spiritual acceptance of God's dealings without bitterness or complaint. That is meekness. What dealings God had with Christ! He was "smitten of God, and afflicted. But he was wounded for our transgressions, he was bruised for our iniquities: the chastisement of our peace was upon him" (Isa. 53:4, 5). So He was chastised of God. The next verse goes further: "The LORD hath laid on him the iniquity of us all." Verse 10, one of the most amazing verses in the Bible, says, "It pleased the Lord to bruise him." I have read those verses for years now, but I cannot even begin to plumb their depths. It was the pleasure of God the Father to bruise God the Son. It was not His pleasure to bruise and break and damn in the depths of hell this guilty sinner! But it was His pleasure to judge His own dear Son in my place. How can I explain that? I cannot. It absolutely transcends all human philosophy and all human reason. Oh, what dealings God had with Christ! They are placed in very sharp focus in the words of Psalm 22, which is, of course, the psalm which begins with Christ's cry on Calvary, "My God, my God, why hast thou forsaken me?" Listen to the words of verses 14 and 15: "I am poured out like water, and all my bones are out of joint: my heart is like wax; it is melted in the midst of my bowels. My strength is dried up like a potsherd; and my tongue cleaveth to my jaws; and thou hast brought me into the dust of death." This is Christ speaking in the silence of His lips but in the eloquence of His soul on Calvary. He says to His Father, "Thou hast brought me into the dust of death." What dealings God had with His Son! And yet He was perfectly meek. "He was oppressed, and he was afflicted, yet he opened not his mouth: he is brought as a lamb to the slaughter, and as a sheep before her shearers is dumb, so he openeth not his mouth" (Isa. 53:7). No complaint. In Gethsemane He cried, "Not my will, but thine, be done." He had said, according to Hebrews 10:7, "I come . . . to do thy will, O God," and He did it.

CHRIST'S GRACIOUS MINISTRY

Having described His humility, the Lord Jesus speaks of His ministry in the second three Beatitudes. We may sum up their message like this: He lived sinlessly, and He loved selflessly. Consider this second set of Beatitudes: "Blessed are they which do hunger and thirst after righteousness. . . . Blessed are the merciful. . . . Blessed are the pure in heart." The first and the third deal with Christ's sinless perfection, while the middle one deals with His deep compassion for wretched sinners. There is the ministry of Christ in a nutshell. His absolute perfection is evident from first to last, and yet that absolute perfection surrounds, as it were, and is manifested in order to, His merciful dealing with sinners.

Jesus said to John the Baptist, as He bade him to baptize Him, "Suffer it to be so now: for thus it becometh us to fulfil all righteousness" (Matt. 3:15). That is how He started out in His ministry. "It becomes us to fulfil all *righteousness."* There is a very interesting thing in the ministry of Christ. At its very beginning (John 2:13-17) He went into the temple and cleansed it. Finding those who sold oxen, sheep, and doves, and the changers of money, He made a scourge of small cords and drove them out. He said, "Take these things hence; make not my Father's house an house of merchandise. And his disciples remembered that it was written, The zeal of thine house hath eaten me up." That was the beginning of His ministry. At the end of His ministry (Matt. 21:12-13) He did exactly the same thing, and He spoke very similar words: "This is a house of prayer. You have made it a den of thieves. Get these things hence." And He drove them out. The Lord Jesus Christ loved righteousness. He had a zeal for righteousness, but everywhere He went He met with sin and hypocrisy. What could be a more telling commentary on Jewish religious life than His words in Matthew 23, when He cried, "Woe unto you, scribes and Pharisees, hypocrites!" Woe! woe! woe!—piling up the woes because of the sin and hypocrisy He found. He was constantly in contact with sin but was perfectly pure in the midst of it all. Peter says that He "did no sin" (I Pet. 2:22). Paul says that He "knew no sin" (II Cor. 5:21). John says, "In him is no sin" (I John 3:5). And Jesus Himself said, "The prince of this world cometh, and hath nothing in me" (John 14:30).

The whole New Testament says He is *pure* and sinless, and yet the sinless Son of God, surrounded by sin, instead of executing flaming judgment, reached out in mercy to poor, guilty sinners. His great design was to work out and establish a perfect righteousness for them—a righteousness that would be perfect in the sight of God and would give them a legal title to heaven. Many people miss the whole meaning of the life of Christ. Some preach as if the only thing that mattered in salvation was the death of Christ. That is far from the truth. I am the last to minimize Christ's death and blood-shedding, but there was no part of His entire life and death that was unnecessary. We have a double obligation to God's law:

to keep its precept, and to pay its penalty when we violate it. Christ our substitute undertook both these obligations. Not only did He die to pay our debt to the broken law and so bear our penalty, He lived to fulfil the precept of the law for us and so provide us with a legal title to heaven. Referring to His last Passover with the disciples, He said, "With desire I have desired to eat this passover with you" (Luke 22:15). In other words, "With the strongest possible yearning I have longed for this final Passover." Why? The Passover was a vivid type of Christ's own death on the cross. Furthermore, the Passover would be turned by Him into the first communion feast, and He would take the bread and the cup and say, "This cup is the new testament, the new covenant, in My blood." The Lord Jesus says, "With great yearning I have anticipated this day." He came with a mighty desire and design to save sinners and to establish righteousness for them. Praise God, He succeeded. Romans 5:18-19 shows that by Adam's sin we were all made sinners. By Christ's obedience and righteousness all believers are counted and constituted righteous in the sight of God. That was the purpose of His coming. This is His mercy.

Mercy is tenderness of heart that is so moved by the wretched condition of men that it acts to remove the cause of their misery and do them good. That is what Christ did. When John the Baptist was in prison, he sent to the Lord Jesus to ask, "Art thou he that should come, or do we look for another?" (Matt. 11:3). Christ's reply was, "The blind receive their sight, and the lame walk, the lepers are cleansed, and the deaf hear, the dead are raised up, and the poor have the gospel preached to them" (v. 5). Wherever there was suffering, the Saviour was there to alleviate it. He was there to wipe away the tears; He was there to heal the broken-hearted. In fact, as He started out in His ministry, the very first Scripture He ever read in public was from Isaiah 61:1, 2: "The Spirit of the Lord is upon me, because he hath anointed me to preach the gospel to the poor; he hath sent me to heal the brokenhearted, to preach deliverance to the captives, and recovering of sight to the blind, to set at liberty them that are bruised, to preach the acceptable year of the Lord" (Luke 4:18-19). That is the mercy of Jesus Christ. I have often thought of that widow leaving the city of Nain on her way to bury her son. I can well imagine her bitter lamentations, but what a difference there was when Jesus halted the funeral procession! Never once did Christ come into contact with death but that death had to yield to the Prince of life. That is what happened at Nain. He stopped the funeral march, called the young man forth, and restored him to his mother. That is mercy.

When the Lord Jesus Christ manifested this powerful mercy, He not only dealt with the surface need, but with the root cause of people's misery. In John 5:14 He says to the man who was healed at the pool of Bethesda: "Sin no more." In John 8:10, 11 He says to the adulterous woman whom He forgave, "Hath no man condemned thee?... Neither do I condemn thee." What words of mercy! As the God of heaven He could have condemned her to the depths of an adulteress's hell, but He says, "I do not condemn you." In other words, "I forgive you. I justify you. But I do not justify you in your sin. I justify you and save you from your sin. Go and sin no more."

That is the mercy of Christ, of whom it was said before His birth, "Thou shalt call his name JESUS: for he shall save his people from their sins." He lived sinlessly, and He loved selflessly. That sums up the ministry of the Lord Jesus Christ. But He lived to die. His cross climaxed His sinless life, which leads us to consider Him as He is portrayed in the final three Beatitudes.

CHRIST'S SACRIFICE FOR SIN

In the third set of Beatitudes we see that Christ made peace at the most awful personal cost. Notice the final three Beatitudes. "Blessed are the peacemakers.... Blessed are they which are persecuted.... Blessed are ye, when men shall revile you, and persecute you." The third set of Beatitudes starts with the thought of peacemaking and ends with the idea of persecution. Here we are brought to the rejection, the suffering, and the death of the Lord Jesus Christ.

He was hated. When He went to His own town of Nazareth at the very beginning of His ministry, the people sought to fling Him headlong over a steep cliff. How many times during His life evil men tried to lay hands on Him, but He passed through the midst of them, for His hour was not yet come. He was hated. He was hunted. He was reviled. The religious leaders knew their Bible, but despite that they looked into the very face of God incarnate and said, "Thou hast a devil." They reviled Him. They said He was mad. They orchestrated His persecution unto death. He was spat upon. He was scourged. Finally, He was crucified.

That is all carnal eyes can see at Calvary, but the truth goes much deeper. Colossians 1:20 says that He "made peace through the blood of his cross." There on Calvary, amid mockery and jeers, amid lashing and cursing, amid all that men and devils could do, the mystery of the ages was being wrought out. God entered upon the scene. There He dealt with His Son as our sin-bearer, and there Jesus Christ wrought salvation. He purchased redemption and reconciled guilty sinners to their God. Satisfying God and justifying the ungodly, He brings them both together by the power of His blood. On the one hand that shed blood pleases God and meets His every demand, while on the other hand it purifies the sinner and meets his every need. Christ the peacemaker brings God and sinners together in perfect reconciliation. He "made peace through the blood of his cross."

Oh, what a price He paid! What suffering He endured! No physical frame, no mental constitution in the history of the world, has known the agony, the suffering, and the distress that were endured by the Lord Jesus Christ. What a price to pay! "The Son of God loved me," said Paul, "and gave Himself for me." In Ephesians 2:14-17 Paul again explores the subject of Christ our peacemaker. He makes three glorious statements: He is our peace; He made peace; He preached peace. Notice the progression.

First, he emphasizes *the person:* "He is our peace." Peace with God is to be found only in Jesus Christ. My friend, you will never have peace with God outside of Christ. There is no peace to the wicked. There is no peace for God to the Christ-rejecter. He may be a religious Christ-rejecter, or a baptized Christ-rejecter, but he cannot have peace while he rejects Christ. Christ alone gives peace with God. There is none other. He is our peace. In the Beatitudes, immediately before the peacemaker is the pure in heart. The order is very significant. It is only because Christ is the pure and sinless One that He can be the peacemaker. None but a sinless Saviour can do guilty sinners good.

"He is our peace." The book of Leviticus gives us a beautiful picture of Christ, who is our peace, in the law of the peace offering. It is altogether unique. In the burnt offering everything was burned; everything went up to God—a type of the fact that Christ's death was first and foremost a satisfaction offered to God. In the peace offering, however, part was burnt on the altar. God was satisfied. Part was given to the priest. Christ was satisfied. And part was eaten by the sinner. The sinner was satisfied. Here is the meaning of Paul's expression, "He is our peace." Christ Himself is the table and the meal around which God the Father, God the Son, and the sinner all sit together. They are all perfectly united in their absolute satisfaction with Jesus Christ. He is our peace. That is the person of the peacemaker.

Second, *the price of peace* is the cross: He made peace. He shed His precious blood. In the darkness of Calvary Jehovah unsheathed the sword of His judgment and justice and plunged it into the bosom of Jesus Christ. His blood was the price of our redemption. I am amazed that men would ever think they could work their way to heaven when it took the blood of Christ to open that way. If you think you will go to heaven because of what you consider good works, you are playing the fool. It is the blood that makes atonement for the soul. It is the blood that brings peace.

The third statement about peace that Paul makes in Ephesians 2 concerns *the preaching of peace:* He "preached peace." The message of Jesus Christ is peace to sinners, peace with God. He came to give this message to Jews and Gentiles. He gives it to you. If you are not saved, you need to be reconciled to God. You need peace with God. God is angry with the wicked every day. The wrath of God abides constantly upon the man who is not saved. The unbeliever is condemned already. You need, therefore, peace between you and God. You need the wrath removed, the sword of justice sheathed. You need the terrors of God's anger and judgment to be taken away and the certainty of heaven to be given in their place. You need peace with God. You also need peace of conscience to face life, death, and eternity. Christ preaches peace. He comes to you with a message of peace, an invitation to be reconciled to God.

We have a great Saviour, an all-sufficient Saviour. In a very simple manner, we have considered His humility, His ministry, and His glorious saving grace. Look to Christ! "See that ye refuse not him that speaketh" (Heb. 12:25). His message is the message you need. His blood can deal with the guilt and the misery of your sin. Therefore call upon Him while He is near. Heed Him while He speaks, and you will find that He is not only *the* all-sufficient Saviour, but *your* all-sufficient Saviour.

CHAPTER FOURTEEN

Christ's Reward

Matthew 5:3-12

E very blessing a Christian enjoys, he enjoys in union with Jesus Christ. The apostle Paul said that we are "blessed . . . with all spiritual blessings in heavenly places in Christ" (Eph. 1:3). No blessing of the covenant of grace can be enjoyed apart from Him. Thus, when we read in Matthew chapter 5 of the blessings conferred upon the people of God, we have to see them as blessings obtained by Christ for His people. We have already considered Christ as the great Original of the virtues listed in the Beatitudes. In this study we will consider the promises attached to those virtues. Just as the Lord Jesus is the great Original of the virtues mentioned at the beginning of each verse, even so He personally, in a pre-eminent way, has entered into the rewards that are listed here as the covenant head of His redeemed people. So, pursuing the theme of Christ in the Beatitudes, we will concentrate on **the glorious accomplishments and achievements of Christ our Saviour.** There are nine Beatitudes, which fall into three sets of three. In the first three Beatitudes, we are directed to consider the humble character of Christ our Saviour; in the second three, His earthly ministry; and in the final three, His reconciling death. Correspondingly, there are three sets of three rewards, or results, appended to these Beatitudes. In the first three (vv. 3-5) the emphasis is upon the sovereignty of Christ. In the second three (vv. 6-8) it is upon the session of Christ at the right hand of the Father. In the third three (vv. 9-12) the great idea is the success of Christ in the entire work of salvation.

THE SOVEREIGNTY OF CHRIST

The first three Beatitudes have attached to them three wonderful statements which emphasize the sovereignty of Christ. "Blessed are the poor in spirit: for theirs is the kingdom of heaven. Blessed are they that mourn: for they shall be comforted. Blessed are the meek: for they shall inherit the earth." When we looked at the commencement of those verses, we saw a reference to the poverty, mourning, and meekness of Christ. We thought of His humble character as the Saviour here on earth. But when we look at the ending of each verse, we see that the lowly man of sorrows is now the King over heaven and earth. The message here is that Christ is the King. God's people can inherit the kingdom only if Christ is the King. That is the message then: He is King.

He is *the King of glory* (Psa. 24:10). Jesus Christ, the man of sorrows, who shed His blood for our redemption, is the centre of all the glory and all the worship of heaven. In the fourth and fifth chapters of the book of the Revelation the Holy Spirit draws aside the veil and lets us see something of the wonderful glory of heaven and of God upon His throne. God has never revealed Himself, either to angels or to men, apart from His Son. There is no place in Scripture where God is revealed to sinners except in and through Jesus Christ. He is the Word of God, the self-expression of God. No creature can ever see God except in Christ. No creature can ever hear God except in His Son. No creature can ever approach God except through Jesus Christ. Even in heaven there is no worship apart from Christ. So when the living creatures and the elders and the myriads of the redeemed worship around the throne of God in heaven, they raise their song to the Lamb of God: "Worthy is the Lamb." He is the centre of all the worship, all the praise, and all the joy of heaven. He is the King of glory. Of course, the world does not yet see that.

> *Our Lord is now rejected*
> *And by the world disowned:*
> *By the many still neglected,*
> *And by the few enthroned.*

Christians see it. The eyes of God's people have been opened, and they acknowledge no real king but Jesus Christ. He is their King. In

Revelation 15:3 He is called *the King of saints*. Paul ascribed to Him the wonderful title "the King eternal." What a name for our blessed Saviour! He is the King of His church. Some clerics have arrogated to themselves such grandiose titles as "princes of the church." Article 10 of the Creed of Pope Pius IV claims that the bishop of Rome is the "Prince of the Apostles." Such proud boasts have no basis in Scripture. As the Westminster Confession of Faith justly remarks, there is no other head of the church but Christ. He is our Prince and Saviour (Acts 5:31), the true King of His church.

And whether men like it or not, He is *the King of earth*. We are told that God's people will inherit the earth. Why? Because Christ as their mediator, their covenant head, has gained that right. He Himself will inherit the earth. He is its rightful King. He is already laying hold of His inheritance. That may sound strange since the world is sunk in sin. Do we not read of the devil as being "the prince of the power of the air"? Is he not the "god of this world"? Yes, he is, but the devil is a usurper. He has no rightful claim to it, and even in this evil age there is a people given by covenant to Christ. Out of all nations and kindreds and tribes and tongues, the Lord Jesus Christ is drawing a people unto Himself, a church of His redeemed. He is saving people from every segment of every society and is bringing them into the society that really matters, the society of the saints. Even now the Lord Jesus Christ is gaining His inheritance. In the covenant of redemption, God gave a people to Christ in order that He may possess them as His possession. No man or devil can rob Him of one whit of His inheritance. Christ the King is almighty to save. He will lose none of His blood-bought people. He has sealed them with His Spirit. They will never be lost. Their King can never be robbed of any part of His inheritance. Not only is Christ now gaining a people out of all the world, but there is coming a day when He will personally come to reign. "The seventh angel sounded; and there were great voices in heaven, saying, The kingdoms of this world are become the kingdoms of our Lord, and of his Christ; and he shall reign for ever and ever" (Rev. 11:15). He shall reign. The crowning day is coming by and by, and those who have enthroned Christ as king will be enthroned with the King when He comes in His glory.

I wonder, are you a rebel against the rightful King? Christ has the kingdom by right. The man of sorrows now is the all-conquering King.

The inheritance belongs to Him. I trust that if you are yet a rebel against God, you will fall on your knees with a broken heart and a submitted will and cry to Christ to set up His throne in your heart. You cannot be a Christian unless Christ is your King. There is much talk about accepting Christ, "praying the sinner's prayer," as if it were a magic formula without any repentance of sin or reference to the Lordship of Christ. It is important that we never lose sight of the simplicity of the gospel or becloud the fact that "whosoever shall call upon the name of the Lord shall be saved" (Rom. 10:13). But calling for salvation is calling on the *Lord*, that is, on Christ the King. Salvation is not a mere form of words. Lip service never got anyone to heaven, and those who refuse to have Christ as their King cannot have him as their Saviour. Call upon the whole Christ. He will save, and He will reign in your soul.

THE SESSION OF CHRIST

The second three rewards in the Beatitudes direct our attention to the session of Christ at God's right hand. "Blessed are they which do hunger and thirst after righteousness: for they shall be filled. Blessed are the merciful: for they shall obtain mercy. Blessed are the pure in heart: for they shall see God." Christ fulfilled the beginning of each of these in His earthly ministry. His reward in His heavenly ministry is seen at the end of each verse. Christ achieved all He set out to achieve and now appears in the presence of God as our great high priest. As our priest, Christ "sees God." Clearly, the emphasis has moved from the earthly ministry to the heavenly.

In our last study we saw Christ hungering and thirsting in this cause of righteousness. *Now we see Him filled.* He is satisfied. Isaiah 53:11 says, "He shall see of the travail of his soul, and shall be satisfied." Everything the Lord Jesus Christ set out to achieve, He did achieve. No desire of Christ is left unfulfilled. No design of Christ is left unperformed. Those are far-reaching statements. All that He set out to do, He did. All that He desired to achieve, He achieved. Every blessing which He sought to purchase for His covenant people, He purchased. Christ is a satisfied, not a frustrated, Saviour. I hear people talking about what the Lord would like to do if only He could. What a travesty of the gospel! Our Saviour is not a conditioned being, but the absolute, eternal, and unconditioned God, by whom everything else is conditioned. I do not believe in a Saviour who would do so much more if only almighty man would allow Him. He shall be filled and satisfied, not disappointed or frustrated.

Then think of His mercy. *He obtained mercy*—not that He was a sinner who needed mercy, for He was the sinless Saviour. But He stood at the head of a company of sinners who needed mercy and obtained every blessing of the evangelical covenant of mercy for them with His own precious blood. David wrote of this: "Thou hast ascended on high, thou hast led captivity captive: thou hast received gifts for men; yea, for the rebellious also, that the LORD God might dwell among them" (Psa. 68:18). That is what the Lord Jesus did. He received gifts—not that He personally needed anything, for as God He is altogether blessed in Himself. But as our mediator He obtained gifts of mercy to give to His people. The Head obtained it for the body. I love the way the psalmist puts it: "Thou hast received gifts for men; yea, for the rebellious also." Gifts for the rebellious!

Our risen Saviour has ascended to the right hand of the majesty on high. *He sees God.* Here is the historical progression of Christ's work. He purchased the gifts; He ascended on high; He sees God. This is an expression of acceptance of Him and His work. It is also a statement of His heavenly intercession. The book of Hebrews lays great emphasis on the exalted Christ and His high-priestly ministry. There is a great misconception among many Christians about the finished work of Christ. People speak of it as if Christ had no further involvement in our redemption once He had said on the cross, "It is finished." That is not what the Bible means by the finished work of Christ. When the Lord Jesus died, He was a priest offering up Himself as a sacrifice without blemish and without spot unto God for us. Now, in heaven, He is fulfilling the other function of the high priest: as our advocate with the Father He is pleading the merit of that perfect finished sacrifice. The sacrificing part is finished, but the once-for-all sacrifice of Calvary is ever fresh as to its on-going power. The blood speaks on our behalf (Heb. 12:24). Hebrews 10:12 puts it very well: "But this man, after he had offered one sacrifice for sins for ever, sat down on the right hand of God." What is He doing there? He is presenting His blood, pleading the merits of His sacrifice. As the forerunner of all His people, He has entered into the very presence of God, guaranteeing that every blood-washed soul will follow Him there. The forerunner will bring in what I may call the after-runners. We will be there. Why? Because Jesus Christ, who died for us, is now presenting His blood. Charles Wesley captured this thought in his immortal hymn "Arise, My Soul, Arise":

> *He ever lives above,*
> *For me to intercede;*
> *His all redeeming love,*
> *His precious blood to plead.*

When Jesus Christ presents His blood to the Father, He is cashing, as it were, the cheque that God the Father issued in the covenant of redemption. He is claiming from His Father everything that His blood purchased. Thus not one blood-bought soul can miss heaven. Jesus Christ our forerunner sees the face of God, and so shall we. His session at the right hand of God is one of the most neglected subjects of New Testament teaching among believers. We have an advocate. We have one who has a legal plea to present before God, and He does so on our behalf. Christ said to Peter: "Simon, Simon, behold, Satan hath desired to have you, that he may sift you as wheat: but I have prayed for thee, that thy faith fail not" (Luke 22:31, 32). That is a wonderful comfort. The devil may be very clever, but he is a fool. He must be, for only a fool would rise up to seek to dethrone almighty God. Sometimes Christians are reduced to a stupor of fear of the devil by well-meaning but misguided preachers. He is a fool, and his folly makes him persist in his endeavour to wreck, ruin, and damn God's redeemed people. Just as he had the arrogance to believe that he could ensnare the Son of God in sin, so he has the arrogance to believe that he can erase the blood-mark from our souls. He would sift us as wheat and destroy us in hell if he could. But Jesus says, "I have prayed for you. I have purchased you with My precious blood. I present that blood before God to claim your entrance into glory. All that I have obtained as your covenant head and Saviour, you will obtain in Me, through Me, and finally with Me." Bless God for the session of Christ at God's right hand.

THE SUCCESS OF CHRIST

The peacemakers "shall be called the children [sons] of God" (v. 9). The persecuted are promised "the kingdom of heaven" (v. 10). The reviled are assured, "Great is your reward in heaven" (v. 12). If all this is true of us, it is even truer of Christ. The final three rewards, therefore, describe the success of Christ. The Christ who is rejected by men is publicly owned by God and has obtained His full reward. *He will be called, or publicly recognized as, the Son of God.* This is the declaration of His deity. Romans 1:4 makes an almost identical statement. He is "declared to be the Son of God with power, according to the spirit of holiness, by the resurrection from the dead." The Holy Spirit of God, when He raised Christ from the dead, declared to men, to devils, and to angels, "This is the Son of God." He declared Him to be God's Son. It is only because Jesus Christ is declared the Son of God that you and I can be called the sons of God. He did not become the Son of God by His resurrection, as some heretics have held. No, the resurrection simply declared it, proved it, and established it in the sight of men.

As the Son of God, *His kingdom is secure.* His is the kingdom of heaven. He has purchased it for all His people. He has opened it to them, and no power of earth or hell can shut it. It is His to give. But there is a further precious thought: Christ's reward will be there. We know that our reward will be there, but so often we overlook the fact that His reward will be there. As the humble, obedient servant unto death, He is rewarded. And what is His reward in heaven? In Hebrews 2:13 He speaks of "the children which God hath given me." He casts His eye over them all and says, "Father, of all those that Thou hast given me, I have lost none." What love, what grace it is that God, the second person of the eternal Trinity, should claim it as His reward that you and I should be in heaven! God's justice would have been served had we been sent to hell. Never for a moment believe the heretical folly that God created us and then saved us because He needed an object for His love. God had the object of His love ever before Him in the person of His Son. There was no inherent necessity in God; there was nothing missing, as if He had the ability to love but no one upon whom He could bestow it. That is not why He created and saved us. Out of the boundless goodness of His heart He created us. Out of His eternal love He wrought redemption for us. Oh, the height and depth of divine love that God the Son has this as His reward, as the crown of His joy, that we should be with Him in heaven! What a success there is in the work of Jesus Christ!

I have called the third section of this study His success. The more I think of it, that is the word that sums up the entire study. Jesus Christ and His glorious accomplishments are evidently set forth throughout. I wonder, have you entered into the finished work of Christ? Have you come to know Him personally and savingly? Is what we have studied more than a doctrine to you? Is He your Saviour, your King, your guarantee of glory? Are you covered with His atoning blood? Have you no other argument for your acceptance with God but Christ and His merit? If you are not saved, I would point you to Christ. I would say to you what an old monk said to Martin Luther many years ago, as the young Luther flagellated himself, bringing himself to the point of death in an effort to gain his own salvation: "Brother Martin, look to the wounds of Jesus." Look to the wounds of Christ. Look to the precious blood. Look to the finished sacrifice. Look, and your soul will live.